PENGUIN BOOKS

A DAY IN THE LIFE OF ROGER ANGELL

Roger Angell is a New Yorker born and bred. His mother, Katharine White, joined the magazine in 1925, the year *The New Yorker* was founded. Angell's stepfather was E. B. White. Although best known and universally acclaimed as a writer on baseball, Angell over the years has written "Talk of the Town" comment pieces, parodies, humorous casuals, and, since 1976, the celebrated annual Christmas verse, "Greetings, Friends." *The New Yorker's* senior fiction editor, Angell has handled the work of John Updike, Ann Beattie, Garrison Keillor, Bobbie Ann Mason, and V. S. Pritchett, among others. He lives in Manhattan with his wife, Carol. He has three children: Caroline, Alice, and John Henry.

A Day

in the Life of Roger Angell

Parodies and Other Pleasures

ROGER ANGELL

A NEW AND REVISED EDITION

PENGUIN BOOKS

PENGUIN BOOKS
Published by the Penguin Group
Viking Penguin, a division of Penguin Books USA Inc.,
375 Hudson Street, New York, New York 10014, U.S.A.
Penguin Books Ltd, 27 Wrights Lane,
London W8 5TZ, England
Penguin Books Australia Ltd, Ringwood,
Victoria, Australia
Penguin Books Canada Ltd, 2801 John Street,
Markham, Ontario, Canada L3R 1B4
Penguin Books (N.Z.) Ltd, 182–190 Wairau Road,
Auckland 10, New Zealand

Penguin Books Ltd, Registered Offices:
Harmondsworth, Middlesex, England

First published in the United States of America by The Viking Press 1970
This expanded edition published in Penguin Books 1990

1 2 3 4 5 6 7 8 9 10

All the selections in this book first appeared in *The New Yorker*, some
in different form.
Charts for "The NCMSB Report" are by Tom Funk.

LIBRARY OF CONGRESS CATALOGING-IN-PUBLICATION DATA
Angell, Roger.
A day in the life of Roger Angell: parodies and other pleasures/
Roger Angell.—A new and rev. ed.
p. cm.
ISBN 0 14 01.4407 2
I. Title.
PS3551.N46D3 1990
814'.54—dc20 90–7388

Printed in the United States of America
Set in Baskerville

Contents

Introduction to the New Edition

This small book was first published twenty years ago, and some of its chapters date back another decade—a Triassic distance away for a collection of humor. Its revival can be looked on as an act of misplaced paleontology or, preferably, as the author's confession of fondness for some short, light pieces that were written swiftly and, as I recall, in high spirits. In a time when humor seems to go out of date more quickly than a quart of low-fat milk, an anthology of stuff from the 1960s may seem no more old-fashioned than one centered on the late Reagan era. The Sixties, to be sure, were stuffed with bad news, but they felt adventurous and sometimes wildly cheerful, as well, and there were books and mornings and headlines that made you want to sit down at a typewriter and try to hold onto some fresh idea that had just come your way.

More than half of these pieces are parodies of some sort, which may in itself give the book a mannered or courtly flavor now. Parody eventually unveils the needle or poignard or rolling pin the author holds behind his back, but it also conveys a compliment, for its target must have a style of its own sufficiently muscular and distinctive to stand up against a poke in the ribs or a puck in the eye. A parody can also be an editorial, and the best parodies—Max Beerbohm on Kipling, Benchley on Dickens, E. B. White on Hemingway, and so forth—turn out to have been about writers (or statesmen or politicians) we had cause to admire as well as distrust. The parodies here that came easiest, as I recall, were those on Lawrence Durrell and Hermann Hesse, because I already knew those strong flavors so well. Parody (as against mimicry) seems to have gone out of fashion, except for occasional bursts on "Saturday Night Live," and one wonders if that isn't because we are short on models and wary of incautious affection: because we care less.

Three chapters from the original edition have been omitted here, because of creakiness, and others have been lightly trimmed or provided with different dropped names or an updated reference here and there—a face-lift that I hope will prove invisible. Most of the pieces were left intact. Some of these, in fact—"The NCMSB Report," about the beginnings of the middle-class cultural saturation; and "Life in These Now United States," which brings back the old *Reader's Digest* at its dopiest— may now work as history, and remind us, perhaps happily, of a milder time and place. (Three new chapters have been added, but these, like all the other works here, have seen prior publication in *The New Yorker*.)

The dangerous mental affliction described in the final chapter, "Ainmosni," eventually subsided in me. Palindromic invention really did damage my nights for a spell in the mid-sixties, and my heroic struggles while attempting simultaneous forward-and-backward thinking should have warned me that my gifts were insufficient to carry the form much farther. Or else I just got too old for such gymnastics. The only recurrence came about ten years ago, when, while watching tennis on television, I detected something odd and damp about the name of the long-time Argentinian pro, Guillermo Vilas. Two hours of my old torture finally yielded "Tennis tips (saliva): Vilas spits in net"— my valedictory, I trust. Other two-way writers have persisted at their labors—among them my friend Allan Miller, the documentary film-maker, who has attained world class. Miller was watching the sixth game of the 1986 Mets–Red Sox World Series when he contrived the brilliant "Not so, Boston"—so deft a summary of the amazing events at hand that I requested and was given permission to use it as the title for my Series piece that fall. Humor does the trick, always.

—ROGER ANGELL

A Day in the Life of Roger Angell

A Day in the Life of Roger Angell

(Mr. Jim Bishop, Author of *The Day Lincoln Was Shot, A Day in the Life of President Johnson,* etc., Grapples Unflinchingly with Still Another Biographee)

6:47 A.M.: The sun, a molten gaseous ball measuring 864,000 miles in diameter, is already up and doing business at its old stand. In Copenhagen, 92,900,000 miles away from the sun and 3,958 miles east of New York's fashionable upper East Side, the sunlight falls straight down like a dropped cymbal, clanging noiselessly off a sidewalk-café table where Jens Nielsen, a fifty-two-year-old bicycle-clip manufacturer, is tucking a snowy napkin into his vest. Mr. Nielsen, obeying certain familiar gastric signals, leans forward and gnashes down pleasurably on his first bite of *smørrebrød:* lunch has begun. At Weather Ship Charlie, Lon. 35°30′ west, Lat. 52°45′ north, in the North Atlantic, the sun at midmorning glowers through a high skin of clouds, casting a swaying gray lozenge of light onto the bunk of Seaman Apprentice Orbert Grummond, who is writing a letter to his mother in East Pharaoh, Kansas. "Dear Mom," Grummond writes after several minutes' cogitation. "No news. This morning we had cirro-stratus at 20,000 feet and chipped beef for breakfast. Yesterday it looked like rain again, but . . ." At this moment, the same sun peeps like a débutante over the ramparts of the abandoned Ruppert Brewery on Manhattan's Third Avenue. Polite morning shadows tiptoe through the quiet streets of the East Nineties, but here, too, there are stirrings, unmistakable signs of significance. A bus clears its throat somewhere to the north. A pigeon, patrolling a narrow third-floor ledge of an old but tasteful brownstone, pauses in its vigil and cocks an amber optic at a half-shaded window. Within the window, in the South-Facing Bedroom of the Walkup, Roger Angell lies face down on the great Sloane's Bed. One massive arm is flung above his head, the hand open in a curiously boyish gesture of ennui. The stern, lightly lipped mouth lies half open. Roger Angell, quite unconscious of Jens Nielsen's lunch and Seaman Grummond's letter, is asleep. Not for him yet is the business of this day, the awful awareness of details, the knowledge that it is *now*. He is lucky.

Others are asleep here too—Mrs. Angell beside her spouse, a daughter in the adjoining Narrow Room—but already the urgent machinery of living has caught up some in the household. The gray, sagacious elder member of the sleeper's personal guard, known by the code name "Daisy," has heard the pigeon's inquiring *"Croo?"* Instantly awake, she lifts her head from its resting place on the bedroom rug. The slitted yellow eyes come open. The pigeon flaps off, and now there is a stirring and irritable sigh from the right-hand side of the bed. The junior guard, code name "Emma," pads in through the half-open bedroom door, eager for assignment, but a warning glance from her superior stops her in her tracks. The Master, a man of Renaissance moods, does not always react favorably to being awakened by a cold nose stuck in his ear. Now there is a magisterial groan from the bed, and the cats leave the bedroom together, walking fast. In both their minds is the knowledge that the Master, when taken by an early-morning mood of scientific inquiry, sometimes indulges his hobby of high-altitude cat-throwing, stubbornly testing his theory that a feline, when lobbed skyward with the proper degree of spin, will not *always* come down on the bed on all fours. At times, while whirling dizzily near the water-stained ceilings of one of the East Side's most extemporary bedrooms, the senior cat has had to remind herself sharply that none of the Master's behavior is intentionally unbearable. She remembers that this is the same man who, on the evening of January 5th, 1964, impulsively slipped her, at her post under the table, a fragrant sliver of roast chicken taken from his own plate. The fact that he claimed no public credit for this gesture, never permitting mention of it to the press, is as typical of the man as is the fact that it was never repeated. Roger Angell has many attributes of "the boss." Generous, large-footed, and joky, he is still no do-gooder or sap. Cats and people in his administration shape up or get out.

Now the South-Facing Bedroom lies silent again, gathering itself for the day to come. Beside the bed, within reach of Roger Angell's hand, lies a telephone instrument, its dial pierced by a circlet of ten finger holes. By picking up the receiver and swiftly rotating the dial with an intelligent forefinger, the man in the Walkup can instantly provide himself with the voices and the immense burden of information necessary to the business of his day—a plumber's answering service, a delicatessen, the correct time. Across the room, on top of a scarred applewood bureau believed by some historians to have seen combat service in the Salvation Army, there lies eighty-seven cents in change, two paper clips, a hairbrush, an American-made rubberoid comb with three teeth missing, and this day's schedule, decisively scrawled the previous evening by Angell himself on the back of an old bank withdrawal slip. The schedule reads: "Gin. Pay Con Ed. Missing pants at cleaner's?" At first glance, it does not look like a busy day, but there is room in it for innumerable new challenges and chapters. Some of the challenges are simmering at this moment within the enormously wrinkled brain still resting on the right-hand pillow. Fifty blocks south of the Walkup and twenty floors up, in the west ventricle of Megalopolis, lies the office of Roger Angell, editor. It and the surrounding offices are empty now, but in a few hours they will be filled by some of the most unforgiving mentalities in America. On the Rectangular Desk rests a matter for decision—a superfluous and possibly dangerous semicolon in a manuscript. This still ticking crisis would understandably tax any human brain, but yesterday Angell studied the problem unwaveringly, chin on fist, before deciding to sleep on it. Now the twisted seedling of the semicolon lies inside the rich loam bed on the pillow, and today, perhaps, the solution will flower.

8:13 A.M.: Roger Angell sits at the Breakfast Table in one of the East Nineties' most eclectic living-dining rooms. The man has already been up for thirty-six minutes. Moving with typical dispatch, he has brushed thirty-two teeth and, with swift, unerring strokes, removed over seven thousand fragments of whisker from chin and jowls. Now it is the time of the eggs. He looks at the eggs, which have been boiled for exactly two hundred and forty seconds, eye to eye. Evidently satisfied, he transfers his attention to the others at the table. The daughter sits to his left, the wife opposite. There is scarcely a face at this table that is not pleasing to him. By example, long silences, and occasional reprisals, he has welded these women into a family. He knows the capacities of his team. Within minutes, the daughter will rise, make her silent adieux, and depart, behind gigantic circular sunglasses, to keep her sullen diurnal appointment with a Smith-Corona upright, deep in the urban pampas. She leaves behind her, in the Narrow Room, a sweetly feminine and American compost. On the bureau, an empty bottle of L'Interdit lies on its side, halfway between an ashtray containing fourteen cigarette stubs and a small straw basket full of hair rollers, unmatched earrings, and buttons bearing arcane contemporary messages of love and defiance. The bedside table is a scene of girlish disarray, reflecting an eager, scholarly mind—*TV Guide, The Olympia Reader,* a dead moth, and an 8-mm-film camera containing an undeveloped but arresting closeup of Allen Ginsberg's left ear. The lady of this room is nineteen, an almost-fledged arrow uneasily at rest within the family quiver.

Absent from the Breakfast Table but warmly present in the bulging filing cabinets of Roger Angell's mind is the other daughter, the younger one, who is at this moment spooning prunes into the two-year-old mouth of a boy currently in her charge at one of Cape Cod's most ineluctable "beach" colonies. At sixteen, she is already a passable bedmaker, a barefoot summer soldier in the ranks of the employed. Now she retrieves a fallen prune from the floor and absently reinserts it in the trusting mouth. The tanned shoulder blades rise and fall in a brief sigh. Even if her father were President of the United States, she would still be here spooning prunes, for the homeliest familial task, when tersely limned, speeds narrative and royalties.

At the table, Roger Angell has thrown himself full tilt into *The New York Times*. Names, issues, torrents of data fly up from the gray columns as the dim, four-eyed gaze, flicking from left to right, absorbs, considers, forgets. At the far end of the table, the lady of the house sips coffee. She is a pretty woman who eats pretty. Soon she too will take her leave, coifed and A-shaped, to meet her economic responsibilities, for everyone in the Angell boat pulls full weight. Within her Gucci pocketbook, the Bonwit's charge plate confidently awaits its noontime airing.

Now the newspaper at the head of the table is lowered briefly, and Angell clears his throat. A thought is on the way to his tongue. The mouth opens. "The Giants," it says, "is dead." Even before the words are out, Angell's quick-striding consciousness has flicked to the next column, where it absorbs more technical intelligence—news of a tennis tournament. Into the Sportsman's mind there floats a clear image of a memorable double fault served by him the previous Saturday, at set point, on a green *en-tout-cas* court eighty-five miles to the north-northeast. The well-netted balls hang in his mind like gasping shad. He rubs his towering forehead and sighs, remembering the aces that once flew off the racquet of a promising editor-athlete named Roger Angell.

The pages of the *Times* rustle and turn. There is a pause at the fashion page, and abruptly the stern face breaks into a creased smile, like a Mark Cross overnight bag being opened. In a soft, pumalike tone, Angell murmurs, "I think Twiggy is a stick." The front door slams; the daughter has gone. The two cats leave the room together, padding on burglar-quick paws. Mrs. Angell is in the kitchen, clashing dishes. The man at the head of the table looks up, puzzled. Breakfast, it seems, is over.

•

9:07 A.M.: The first Gristede delivery bikes rattle up Madison Avenue on their life-giving rounds. In Copenhagen, Jens Nielsen nervously paces the worn carpeting of his dusty office. On Weather Ship Charlie, Seaman Grummond stares irritably off at the horizon and bites his nails. Both are waiting to resume their parts in this drama of the present. Is it possible that they have been forgotten? Roger Angell is alone in the Walkup. Wearing pale-fawn boxer shorts, he stands in front of the kaleidoscopically jumbled tie rack inside the closet door of the South-Facing Bedroom. Low-key reps, rich silks, brightly checked ginghams come before his gaze. This is the time of the tie, and Angell the Dandy does not hurry. There is reputation to be sustained in this area, for Roger Angell knows that a junior reporter, hopelessly overmatched in a struggle for office hardworsted supremacy, was once heard to mutter petulantly, "No one has *ever* seen the tops of Angell's socks." Today, however, the lightning of decision does not strike. Yawning, Angell shuffles to the bureau and begins to pull on a clean shirt. One arm is in the shirt when his eye falls on the scribbled day's calendar. Now the lean-shanked frame swings into action. He picks up the telephone and dials the dry cleaner's. The voice on the other end recognizes the caller and replies at once, ready for action. Inefficiency is raw skin at the Walkup.

Like many middle-aged literary men, Angell is unafraid to descend to the use of plain language in time of stress. "Hey," he rasps, the voice rising dangerously, "where the hell are my gray pants?"

Accustomed to brusque demands from this quarter, the voice on the phone suggests a possible solution. The tall instigator of the inquiry demurs flatly. The voice placates, rephrases, suggests. Angell, the half-on, half-off shirt flying behind him, strides to his wife's closet and finds there, swatched in Pliofilm and hidden between two freshly pressed dresses, the erroneously placed garment. He returns to the phone. No social amenities are brooked at such a time. "Right," he snaps, and hangs up.

Roger Angell has been awake for an hour and forty minutes, and one-third of the day's calendar has already become history. Now a weariness, a mood of introspection typical of sensitive men, comes over him. It seems to him that the knuckle of the day has already been gnawed. He spots the gawky, half-dressed figure in the bedroom mirror, and looks away. Unaccountably, the sleeved arm comes out of the shirt. The shirt is thrown aside. Angell sits on the bed and studies his Gothic feet. The man on the bed considers the issues that lie in wait for him. He thinks of the semicolon still dangerously coiled on the snake pit of the Rectangular Desk. He remembers the unresolved riddle of the necktie. Once, the man in the Walkup would have charged pell-mell at these problems, but slowly, steadily, he has come to accept the truth that everything cannot, or at least need not, be accomplished at once.

The wise gray guard slips noiselessly into the room and takes up her post on the rug. She watches while the Master lies back on the tastefully flowered bedspread. Then, with an infinitely delicate gesture of contempt, she lowers her head onto her paws. Across the room, the great feet are swung up onto the bed and comfortably crossed. Now there is a sigh. Now a soft snore rises into the morning air. Roger Angell's day—or certainly more than enough of it—is over.

Your Horoscope

(More Unsolicited Guidance from Out There)

Taurus (Apr. 21-May 21)

With Venus ascendant and frozen pork-belly futures holding firm, this is a week for modest household chores. Unkink and clean all shoelaces, not overlooking the lacing on your football. Recaulk the dog's water dish, the tank on the Water Pik, etc. Toward the end of the week, chair casters may be inspected in relative safety. Because of an enigmatic (or quietly amused) aspect of Mercury, it would be wiser not to get dressed before nightfall.

Gemini (May 22-June 21)

Sorry, Gemini people, but still no advice for you. Eleven weeks now and still not a word from the Stars for this dormant house! Oh, well, things are bound to start popping soon. Meantime, try not to do anything at all.

Cancer (June 22-July 22)

A confused period for you normally ebullient Crabs. Purely social occupations will help keep your mind off insomnia, erasers, and eastbound watercraft. Damp bathing suits may prove annoying on Tuesday, but try to keep your composure at all costs. Some rumpling of the eyebrows may be observed upon arising. An elderly terrier will be thinking about you over the weekend.

Leo (July 23-Aug. 23)

Your best week of the entire year for sheer recklessness. Obey that wiggy impulse! Vault subway turnstiles, dress up in your wife's clothes, tell off a policeman, coat yourself in peanut butter—it doesn't matter, for the Stars say this is your time to howl! A meditative period will descend late in the week, when you may wish to consult legal and medical experts.

Virgo (Aug. 24-Sept. 23)

Those not born under this sign would do well to visit all their Virgo friends before 4:20 P.M. on Monday, but to stay well away thereafter. As for you Virgos—well, astrology is still a difficult science, and maybe we're reading these signs wrong, ha, ha! Good luck to you all.

Libra (Sept. 24-Oct. 23)

A time for inwardness and mental housecleaning. Try to rid your mind of excess baggage. Forget about the Diet of Worms. Forget factoring, the cambium layer, Up with People!, and Sibyl Colefax. Get rid of the Rock of Chickamauga, the color of Ventnor Avenue, and the words of "Three Itty Fishies." Throw out Ipana Toothpaste, the auteur theory, and "anent." Try never to think about tundra. What a lot of trash you've been carrying around in the old bean! No wonder you can't make any money.

Scorpio (Oct. 24-Nov. 22)

Mars will be entering this house shortly after lunch on Tuesday, so you Scorpios, already habitually suspicious, would do well to double your guard in this period. If your friends have been whispering about you in the past, just think what they're saying now! Laundrymen and Celts may try to bilk you, possibly through the mails. An agent of a Balkan power, perhaps posing as a close relative, will try to blow nerve gas through your telephone receiver while you sleep. Next week will be worse.

Sagittarius (Nov. 23-Dec. 21)

All you Archers—so good-looking, so impetuous, so lovably harum-scarum—have been making a perfect hash of your lives ever since the moon slipped off your cusp way back in March, 1964. Time to come down to earth! This week, try to study some modest, everyday object and appreciate its true nature. Study one of your thumbs, for instance. Not the handsomest of all your fingers, perhaps, but one that does the job, day in and day out, without fanfare or vaingloriousness. See how wrinkled it has grown around the knuckle, but with never a word of complaint. You are lucky to have stubby Mr. Thumbkin (a typical Gemini) working for you, and you might do well to emulate his patience. If you were a dog or a fox, your thumb would be way up by your wrist somewhere, and absolutely useless. What a lesson for us all!

Capricorn (Dec. 22-Jan. 20)

Rickey Henderson, Senator Mondale, Marilyn Horne, J. D. Salinger, Henny Youngman, Phil Donahue, Bo Diddley, and President Nixon were all born under this sign, which rules the knees. The best guide to your week is to watch these fellow-Capricorns closely, for if things go well for them, they will go well for you, too. If they all have a terrible week—hamstring pulls, blocked legislation, tonsillitis, intrusive visitors, no laughs, etc.—so will you, in your own tiny way. You may find it difficult to discover much in common with each and every one of these Goat people, but that's the way astrology works, so stop complaining.

Aquarius (Jan. 21-Feb. 19)

Persons born under Aquarius are restless, indolent, fond of water sports, pleasing, and agreeable. Their greatest fault is procrastination. This will be a fine week for you to mooch around the house quietly, smoothing over family arguments and making friends with the milkman. Take a nap or look out the window for a while. Maybe you could get in a little surfing. On the other hand, why don't you wait and go surfing *next* week? What the hell.

Pisces (Feb. 20-Mar. 20)

This week climaxes a series of highly favorable indications for fish and Fish people. Go to the aquarium, take up fly-tying, buy a pair of guppies. Try codfish balls for breakfast—delicious! On Friday, before the onset of your coming counter-period of drought, why not throw a mammoth "Fish Fry"? Invite Hamilton Fish, Bob Trout, Ben Pollack, Dick Bass, Jean Shrimpton, Aldo Ray, Hulan Jack, Congressman Pike, etc. How they will laugh when they all "get it"!

Aries (Mar. 21-Apr. 20)

The stars tell us that during the coming six to eight weeks the Palestinian Liberation Organization will be overthrown by a Mormon clique; two members of the Quebec Nordiques will be unmasked as C.I.A. agents; Liverpool will be ravaged by locusts; Akron, Ohio, will slide into the Atlantic Ocean (you can't argue with the Stars); the International Monetary Fund will be rocked by a Jimmy Swaggart-type scandal; and an oil slick will imperil the Wollman Memorial Rink. In view of the world-shaking nature of these impending events, how can you pushy, invariably selfish Rams keep asking astrologists for help with your petty personal affairs? Enough, already! Can't you see we're busy?

In the Dough

Virginia Hardy's Story Writing Contest!

Virginia Hardy's Oven invites all patrons and friends to enter our Short Story Contest. At least one and as many as three stories will be selected each month for inclusion on Virginia Hardy's Oven pie boxes. (We print and distribute over a million boxes per year!) The author of each story selected will receive a prize of fifty free pies at any Virginia Hardy's Oven. Stories should be between 750 and 1250 words long, and, of course, suitable for general audiences. Please include a brief description of yourself suitable for our "About the author" section . . .

—Notice on a pie box.

Mrs. Ishbel Carrington Shute
Fiction Editor
Mother Melmoth Pastry Pantries, Inc.

Dear Mrs. Shute:
Am enclosing proofs of "Queen of Hearts" in haste to catch deadline. Please restore and stet the lines inexplicably deleted by you on galley 2, from "Now, in delicious disarray . . ." through ". . . a glimpse of regal bosom, charmingly dusted with an inadvertent dab of flour, that rose and fell, here within the sweet warmth of the summer kitchen, in quickened tempo. Knavish Jack, suddenly apant, stepped forward from the shadows," etc., etc. These sentences, rough and hand-hewn though they may appear, are essential to the ensuing chase scene, and also serve to render the Queen less distant and, yes, more earthily female, thus preparing your readers for the sensual reconciliation after the recapture of the purloined tarts. Please, dear Madam, stay

your avid blue pencil here, recalling that an artist has pondered, sampled, and weighed each staple noun, each zesty adjective, each pinch of comma in his desire to create beauty at once nutritious and lighter than air. Exactly, in brief, like one of your master bakers.

Speaking of which, your payment for "Cherry, the Cobbler's Daughter" arrived today. Thanks for home delivery. And for the Lemon Meringues—they are *scrumptious!* We still have twenty-one Squash pies and eleven Boston Cream left over, thanks to your other recent acceptances, so the children welcomed this change of menu.

A new effort goes off to you tomorrow. I am dipping toe, tremblingly, into the icy seas of biography—the pie as history, so to speak.

Yours ever,
Duane McConakree

Mr. Duane McConakree
Iowa City, Iowa

My Dear Duane (if I may):
Tremble no more. You have triumphed afresh, huzza! Not since the initial felicities of "Horner!" (now in its *sixth* edition—Rhubarb), or perhaps since I first cast a furtive tear over the joys of your "Shoo-Fly: A Rustic Romance," have I been so caught up, so held as I was by "Karl Robert Nesselrode, Lad of Old Russia." You have done us honor once again, and payment of fifty pies (Chocolate Nesselrode, natch) goes to you out of tonight's baking, plus a deserved bonus of thirty Old-Fashioned Southern Pecan. Don't thank us, please. The privilege of presenting your seemingly inexhaustible *oeuvre* upon our humble cardboard palimpsests is reward aplenty. I await your next

Hungrily,
Ish

Dear Ish:
Enclosed find "Priscilla's Punkins"—in time, I trust, for a quick closing on an appropriate mid-November pub. date. It seems a

graceful effort, but I find it more and more difficult to judge. To tell the truth, I am bored to near dementia by this facility of mine, this Niagara of pastry puffs, but my weird old muse stands over me, rolling pin in hand, and I can but obey.

Assuming acceptance again, may I request payment this time in a separate flavor? LaVerne and little Zachary hate pumpkin. Anent which, and at the risk of jarring our perfect author editor symbiosis, I wish to suggest a modest but commonsensical alteration in this matter of payment. This morning, during a thorough inspection of the dangerously overloaded shelves in our kitchen and laundry room, plus the teetering contents of three second-hand cupboards now doing makeshift service on the sun porch, I counted thirty-eight remaining Nesselrode pies, twenty-two Pecan, one Squash, four Lemon Meringue, forty-nine and a half Rhubarb (not, in truth, a terribly popular item here), eleven kuchen, one and one-quarter Coconut Cream, fourteen Butterscotch Chiffon, and sixteen assorted stale, crumbled, or unidentifiable, which I confiscated. This accounting does not include the nine dozen-odd pies that LaVerne has unloaded, for the merest fraction of their value, on our Eagle Discount manager and other surly local merchants, in lieu of the more common form of specie. We are, in short, amassing a corner in pies, and the essential flavor I now crave is Old Legal Tender.

These are sere times for writers of short fiction, God wot, but A. Daptable is my middle name. This hack, for one, is almost ecstatically grateful for the evidences of high literary seriousness to be found in (or on) your unusual publication. I write only in order to eat and to fill the four gaping maws within my nest, and all I ask, Ish, is a little less damned efficiency in this process. The mantle of George Horace Lorimer has fallen on the shoulders of your chef, yet this seems an insufficient excuse for the conversion of my home into a museum of *pâtisserie*. I am attempting to phrase this proposal in businesslike terms, eschewing mention of the increasingly doughy complexion of my loved ones, the Zeppelin-like recent configuration of my once lissome LaVerne, and the piteous cries that arise from the family dining table when yet another meal commences, continues, and concludes with implacably wedge-shaped helpings.

Send cabbage, Mother Melmoth!

Duane

Cher Maître:
Accept the greeting, for you are not, as you have lately claimed, the Irving Wallace of Pie Writers but rather the Maupassant—nay, the Balzac. Truly, I had not guessed that our square, even boxy, little journal was ready for a tale of miscegenation and the ironies of a postbellum plantation romance, but today's submission, "Brown Betty," has quite taught me otherwise. In short, a triumph! There is even more good news, for Howard Johnson's has just chosen our Tarte aux Fraises (with your classic "Simple Simone" as text) as its Pie of the Month for August, which assures rich returns for all. By the way, our people in Accounting tell me that cash payments are a no-no, but they have promised to include three dozen Beef-and-Kidney in your next royalty, thus alleviating the little dietary problems you mentioned. Glad to be of help!

Luv,
Ish

Ish:
I give up. Can your treasurer be wholly unaware that it has been some little time since Western man inched out of the long darkness of the barter system and into the sunshine of freely redemptive currencies? Has he not had the news that U.S. Steel no longer pays its dividends in ingots? Has he ever tried settling his telephone bill with a half-dozen Banana Cream Tortes? Has he attempted to write lean, rivet-hard prose after a breakfast of Apricot Pan Dowdy (cold) and *réchauffée* Mince à la mode? I warn you, a man can be whipped just so far.

LaVerne, displaying a mobility quite uncharacteristic of most siege howitzers, has transformed our driveway and garage into a used-pie lot ("Drive In 'n' Nibble!"). Commercial response seems initially discouraging, but I am not absolutely sure about this, because the lady has not spoken to me these past three weeks.

I enclose, God forgive me, three new efforts—my last to you for some little time to come. I am determined to widen my market or quit this mad métier utterly.

Duane

Duane Dear:
Your threats do not convince me, for genius is simply not free to opt out. Conrad and Dostoevski also railed against the lonely dark, and yet did their duty in the end. I can hardly choose among the three new *contes* (a baker's dozen dozen's-worth of fresh pies for thee!), but "A Tragedy in Custard" was certainly the most surprising. Who but you could wring pathos from the plight of a Keystone pie-thrower with bone chips in his elbow?

Onward!
Ish

Kabibble:
Back again, as you foresaw. My attempts to escape the thrall of piedom have come to nothing. I have the rejection slips before me—from the Hasta Luego Chili Corp., Hedda Gobbler Frozen Turkey Parts, Old Shiloh Bourbon, Tweetie-Cat Pet Dinners, etc. A clean sweep, even including my delicate Petrarchan sonnet, "Con Formaggio," which came back on an instant ricochet from the Molto Buona Pizza people. Call me mad, for I am henceforth forever pied.

I am at least alone. Last Thursday, at five in the morning, our garage departed the premises in an eruption of noise and flame strongly reminiscent of a Cape Kennedy liftoff. Talk about pie in the sky . . . Dawn disclosed the neighbors' topmost tree branches and most distant shrubbery prettily festooned with parts of variously flavored tarts, cobblers, meringues, and down-home deep-dishes, the whole resembling a direct hit on a Sicilian antipasto-works. Not a bad metaphor, in truth: I take this as a veiled warning from some local pastry-shop owner possibly miffed at our new venture in cut-rate pie-peddling. Later in the morning, while attempting to nail some pie plates over a gaping hole in our roof, I witnessed the final and not unexpected decampment of Herself and the bairns in the family auto—off, I don't doubt, in simultaneous search of a better-balanced diet and father. From my vantage point, the tableau resembled a Green Bay Packer making off with a shipment of medicine balls.

Alone now. My brain is but mincemeat, my soul chiffon, yet still shall I fight my way free . . .

D.

Dear Duane:

Do I detect a new, darker side to your prose? Why, I wonder. "Ludwig's Journey," for instance, has me a mite puzzled. It is, of course, a stunning theme: Ludwig, an ancient immigrant to our shores, forms an irresistible longing for one last slice of Bavarian Cream pie homemade in his own native Bavarian hamlet. Exchanging his life savings for a steerage ticket, he reaches Europe and then falls victim to a gang of ruffians in Le Havre, who rob him of his all. Nothing daunted, he presses on by foot, hobbling half the breadth of the Continent in hopes of that last one memorable mouthful. Winter falls, and our aged hero becomes lost in the Black Forest. He struggles on, the vision of Bavarian Cream before him. At last, he climbs the final mountain escarpment between himself and his goal, and is swept up in an avalanche that deposits him, more dead than alive, at the very door of his village piemaker.

All well up to here, Duane. A crackerjack pie tale, in fact. But now you begin to lose me. With gnarled and frozen knuckle, Ludwig taps on the baker's door. It opens. Prone, the battered old gentleman whispers his dear request. But what is this? *"Nein,"* says your baker bluntly. "Ve are all out off der Bavarian Cream." Ludwig shrugs his shoulders and replies, "O.K. How about a slice of Pineapple-Cheese?" Finis. I mean, ? ? ?

Well, Duane, we have had a knockdown, top-level edit hassle here, but thanks to your Ish, I must admit, "Ludwig's Journey" will run as is. I persuaded the other minds here that the story represented a passing, Beckett-like strain in your otherwise un-ambiguous work, and that we owed you at least one such fugue. One, I might add, and no more. Obscurantism pushes no pies.

Ish

Dear Ish:
Sorry about that. I trust this will make amends—a simple re-telling of Shakespeare's "Titus Andronicus."

Duane

Dear Duane:
Welcome back, kind sir! Not one of us here had ever read or seen "Titus Andronicus," and so hadn't an inkling that it con-cludes, so surprisingly and pleasingly, in a pie-eating scene. I *love* old-fashioned blood-and-thunder mellerdrama. We are run-ning it on our big Washington's Birthday Cherry Special—a rush job in time for the holiday. Thanks and congrats!

Ish

P.S. It's of no matter, but what is the flavor of that pie that the disguised Andronicus serves to Tamora in the final scene?

Mrs. Shute:
I have before me a box of your Washington's Birthday Cherry Special, with my little tale from the Bard well featured on the obverse. I feel again the deep satisfaction that sometimes overtakes even the most experienced author when he reads his own work and in all honesty must whisper to himself, "Oh, well done!"

You ask—ha-ha!—for the recipe of Titus's homemade, ex-tremely deep-dish pie. I note—hoo, haw! *gnick-gnick!*—that you do not also inquire about the whereabouts of Tamora's children, the rascally Chiron and Demetrius, who are so oddly and inex-plicably absent from the dessert course. Think, Madam. *Hmm.*

What is the new, tangy flavor? Can phylophagia push pies? How do you like them apples, Mother Melmoth?

I have written my last! Today I begin my new permanent employment, as an artist with the graphic-arts division of the U.S. Bureau of the Budget.

Ish, fare thee well.

Duane

Ivy

(Evidences of a Severe Literary Syndrome Experienced after Absorbing, in One Delicious Gulp, the
Four Alexandrian Novels, *Justine, Balthazar,
Mountolive,* and *Clea,* by Mr. Lawrence Durrell,
to Whom Is Offered a Deep Levantine Bow)

Landscape-Tones: thumbsmudged grays athwart the walls of the
unswept corridor: fuchsine pink of the floorward-pointing arrow
above the door of the awaited, chain-rattling elevator. Mud-
spatter tans and greens on the okapi flank of the evening taxi.
Remembered lilac mauves in the flecks of her eyes as she lay,
softly sighing over some imagined slight, in her charming accustomed attitude of exhaustion. Bruise-purples on the shoulders of the wheeling pigeons, short scimitars slicing the white
sky of this too-Western littoral.

Copernicus, the milkman, has been missing for a week. His
last delivery consisted of two pints of strawberry yoghurt, a gnos-
tic warning of his disaffection. Another mystagogue gone from
the Cabal.

Cat-dust afloat between the ramparts of the timeless, senec-
tuous tenements, caught and made golden by a random sunshaft,
and below, in the dry jungle of smashed hedges and stillborn
philodendron, ravaged by the sneakered *fellaheen* of the quarter,
the animals themselves, self-consumed by the yellow hunger of
their ancient eyes. She used to watch them from our back window, my sweet voyeuse, her entire body quivering in sympathy

for their loneliness, and I would sense myself abandoned again. Ivy, the Nefertiti-eared. How can I face her now?

Crumbie, the subway motorman, sensed the truth, or the lie, in our relationship. Once, asprawl in my sling chair, his vast belly comfortably between his knees, and his humorous, rheumy, jongleur's eyes alight with the inner wisdom, the thesaurian omniscience that all my acquaintances seem to possess, he waved one of his great cuffed gloves at her as she lay asleep beside me, her head on my lap. "You think she loves you, don't you, *mon vieux?*" he said, his voice rumbling out of the caverns of his chest like an onrushing E train. "Love is your obsession. Your old noddle whirls with it day and night, the needle scratching out the same meretricious *javas*. My poor littérateur, you confuse possession with passion, convenience with adoration. Mark my words, Aeneas, you will do your innocent Dido a great hurt one day." Titubating slightly in his chair, he reached down between his feet for his glass, which was characteristically empty (he had a great thirst for the native elixirs), and held it out toward me. "You got any more *phabst,* buddy?" he said, smiling wickedly.

He was right, of course. I knew it, thought I denied it thumpingly; even at the height of my shrill recusance, I could hear a piquant, subterranean *scritch-scritch!* within me—the rat-gnawings of suspicion and betrayal. How could I doubt the love of one who lay so innocently beside me now, one who had often rewarded me with a trusting, housewifely snore as I read aloud to her from my annotated volumes of de Sade and Rider Haggard? But for every trust there is a countering suspicion within us, love's antimatter. I remembered mysteries, evasions. From whom did she obtain such a gift as that uncut, sanguineous, Persian-red *bifteck* I saw her carrying, wordlessly ecstatic, across the croquet lawn of the Summer Embassy in Katonah early one Sunday morning? I never dared ask her. I have even suspected that she and Cloya might love each other. A bat thought, brushing my face in the dark. Once I surprised Cloya proffering her a Necco wafer, and sometimes on winter evenings I have intercepted a look between them, a feminine arrow of understanding

and commiserating sympathy. Ouf! What confusions, what fer-
berian profundities!

Crumbie was still watching me. Could he know what evil surprise I had planned for Ivy? Guiltily, I looked down at her
seamed, dew-lapped muzzle, the beloved profile of *ma jolie laide*,
and then I awakened her and she and I played gaily before him,
as if to exorcise, with her rubber bone, the witch truth that we
all recognized. I remember that as we romped together, two
acolytes of love hurrying through the enforced rituals of our
order under the wise eye of an aged archimandrite, Crumbie
murmured, "How typical of you to own a bulldog. Especially a
bitch. Outrage is your forte, as are antipodes. Thus your effem-
inate battler, your womanish Hercules. Of course, she is far too
good for you."

Even as he spoke, there fell a sudden bumbling of thunder
from the flat, sullen sky without—an ominous throat-clearing of
the gods preceding the passing of some awful sentence. And
now the deed is done, the sentence executed, and I must go this
afternoon to Dr. Balsamic's establishment and face Ivy, she who
understood almost nothing (no more than the impatient reader
of some significant palimpsest) of what the hell was going on
between us.

Season of the stocking-ladder. Winter-clank in the starved
steampipes. Faint effluvium of mixed vetiver and pot from the
empty marzipan jar. Rain squalls in the West Fifties, dappling
the roofs of the versicolorate sports cars clustered like rank,
overripe fruit in their dusty orchards. Cloya's face seen upside-
down in her full Martini glass, an avid water-lily.

Pierrepont, the gharry driver, is dead, possibly by his own
hand. He was found slumped over the wheel of his cab, the coils
of his *narguileh* twisted tightly about his aristocratic, Hittite neck.
He had been a great womanizer, but he had been forced to deny
his appetites cruelly. He confessed to me once that he suffered
agonies from couvade and that his analyst (his "psyche-twist," as
he called him) had warned him that he might not survive another
confinement. Sad.

Aleicester, the poet, has at last finished the mighty palindrome that has entirely engaged his attention for the past eight years. Cloya brought it to me at dawn last Tuesday and I read it through in six hours, all the way from its brave, Homeric opening statement "T. Eliot, top bard, notes putrid tang," to the great dying fall of its final line, ". . . Gnat-dirt upset on drab pot toilet." Cloya tells me it will probably never be published; Aleicester, half mad with his vision, has already wrangled with his publisher, claiming that since the work can be read backward as well as forward he must receive double royalties. Ironic end to one so talented, so bored.

Did I say "too-Western littoral" earlier? Odd! Just this morning I received another communication from Pinchbeck, the novelist, in which he urges me to move eastward. Near the end of this typically assertive document—a high-heaped interlinear correcting certain literate but misconceived comments I had scrawled in the margins of a fugitive work by Rhodmek Kün, the old bard of this narrow, fluminose island—he writes: "Novelists, like horticulturists, must find the proper climate for their little crop of hybrid conceits. If you persist in planting your lush tropical blooms by the sidewalks of a Hyperborean stone city, you will not be entitled to the luxury of surprise or hurt when preoccupied residents turn coldly away from your finest blossoms muttering, 'They don't even look real.' Your own verbgarden, your overmulched nouns, require a feverish Levantine sun, the swollen profligacies of some Eastern delta. Plant your flowers there—in Smyrna, Aleppo, or Alexandria—let them burgeon in all their premeditated brilliance, and *then* watch the tourists trample your borders! See them sniff, note the shocked delight in their eyes as they ogle each purple stalk, each velvet petal, each naughty stamen, and listen to them as they exclaim, 'How lovely, how wicked, how *true!*' "

Pinchbeck is listenable, of course, but I must confess that I suspect him of jealousy. For one thing, he writes so much like me—implacably Gongoresque, logorrheac to a fault. And then, Copernicus has told me that Pinchbeck once indulged in a bitter public outburst against my concept of the novel as a five-sided continuum—the quincunx book, with four characters (or four volumes) spinning in orbit about the fixed center dot of events, like a die flung down on the green baize table of truth.

I must leave now: she will be waiting. The skin over my temples feels tautly stretched—a certain warning of the onset of *cafard*. It takes me forever to get going these days; one might even suspect me of wishing to inflate the meaning of each action, however trivial or fascinating, through cunctation and quiddity.

Out, then, again into the streets. I turn westward, toward the sun, stumping bravely toward Dr. Balsamic's antiseptic couloirs. Mica-sheen from the minarets of the Squibb Building. Below the conflagration of afternoon sky, below the great Weehawken Corniche, the seared, exhausted traffic-swarm, thrilling the belly with the blare of its impatient horns. Squadrons, platoons, entire divisions of pedestrians, package-bearing, newspapered, come clicking toward me, and I notice again how blurred, how impalpable they all seem in the ambient mistral that blows across this city at all seasons from the slopes of Mt. Simile. On the corner, Gepetto, the bearded convert, winks to me as he hurries past on his way to evensong—the Copt on the beat.

I come at last to the address, pass under the chaste, fly-specked sign ARISTOTLE BALSAMIC, D.V.M., and step into the white-walled foyer and the clean, masochistic scent of iodoform. The Dravidian receptionist ushers me into Balsamic's empty consulting room, where I sit briefly, listening to the yelps and bayings of hell that fall faintly here upon my abashed ears. Palpitant, I hear a step and a shuffle without, and they enter, Balsamic resembling a sleepy-eyed snowy owl in his sterile gown, and Ivy almost hidden behind him, her head low.

No bandage. I had expected bandages. My waif is thinner, etiolated by her experience, but when she sees me her gazelle eyes light up bravely. But she does not throw herself into my arms in her customary abandoned *abrazo*. It is as I had known it would be: forgiveness was too much to expect.

I must speak. "How is she, Doctor?"

"Fine," Balsamic says. "No complications. You can take her home now."

"But then what?" I cry out. "What will she think of me for putting her through all this? I mean, what about the *spirit*, the inner maelstrom? Isn't there danger of post-operative synecdoche?"

Balsamic regards me skeptically, looking like—well, like a skeptical doctor. "Listen," he says wearily, "it was perfectly routine. It's normal to spay a dog of her age. I recommended it, and I'm sure I was right."

I take the leash from him and make one more effort. "Doesn't it mean *anything* to her?"

"Not a blessed thing. Oh, if she seems to have any trouble sleeping tonight, you might slip her a Bufferin, but that's all. In a few days she'll have forgotten all about this." He must perceive some vestigial shimmer—could it be disappointment?—in my eyes, for he steps forward and places a friendly, scrubbed, Philistine hand on my arm. "Look, fella," he says in his emollient baritone, "you writers, particularly you vocabulary-enrichers, ought to go easy on yourselves. All this high-class suffering and speculating, I mean. You're so damned sure that everybody is chock-full of passion and guilt and memory and all like that, when most of the time—almost all the time, if you ask me— they're not thinking of anything but their next can of Ken-L-Ration. Keep that in mind—O.K.?"

I nod, and Ivy and I take our leave. Outside, darkness has veiled the aged face of the courtesan streets, and the buildings above us cast down an autumnal pollen of yellow lights. The leash slack between us, we turn automatically and prophetically toward the East, each wincing faintly from our interior wounds. We are both exhausted, and no wonder.

AFTERWORD TO *"Ivy"*

Lawrence Durrell may be surprised to learn that he is not the only British author to have been slighted in this slipshod forgery. The visionary palindromist introduced above as "Aleicester, the poet" is modeled not on one of Mr. Durrell's maimed romantics but on Mr. Alastair Reid, the distinguished Scottish poet and author, who wrote the two-way lines quoted here. His "mighty palindrome," while actually requiring something less than six hours to read, deserves to be quoted in full, for it is the most stimulating long-distance shuttle in our language: "T. Eliot, top bard, notes putrid tang emanating, is sad. I'd assign it a name: 'Gnat-dirt upset on drab pot toilet.'"

Exemplary readers who persist to the final chapter of this book will find Mr. Reid still smiling graciously and anonymously as he is again victimized in exactly the same way. Few authors have displayed equal courage when confronted with such a reckless kleptomania.

The Floto Letters

(Correspondence in the Lindsay Flavor)

Dear Mayor Floto:

Starting this new "Vox Pop" letters column in the newspaper so citizens can write to you direct about the conditions of their city is nothing but another cheap "politician's trick," but just the same I think I will send you my "beef." Nothing runs anymore in this town, and that goes especially for the Scarlatti Fountain out on West Inglenook (near where I live), which is a disgrace. The pools are all dried and cracked and full of trash, the water pipes and nozzles are rusted away, and somebody has broke off the composer's nose and part of the harp that belonged to the Muse. Another nice old part of the city ruined and another insult to the Italian people. What are you going to do about it?

Burned Up

Dear Burned:

As you may know, the problem you mention has already been dealt with. The party or parties unknown who stole the Scarlatti Fountain last Thursday night are still at large, but Police Chief Hackbart assures me that his department has several promising leads and that the miscreants will soon be brought to justice. In the meantime, decent citizens like yourself can find some comfort in the knowledge that there is a very poor current market for late-nineteenth-century rococo sculpture, and, likewise, that the cost and trouble of repairing, installing, and furtively operating a fifty-eight-foot vertical-spray fountain will detract considerably from any private aesthetic comfort these despoilers may have envisaged. I believe that this entire episode constitutes a lesson for us all, illustrating the value of patience in solving urban problems. Frankly, the question of what to do about the decaying Scarlatti Fountain had been allowed to hang fire for some time, ever since a deadlocked hearing of the Municipal Arts Board in 1927. Up to last week, the matter still seemed hopeless, yet today it has been entirely cleared up—cleared up, I may point out, at no cost to the taxpayers. As Scarlatti himself might have said, *Allegro non troppo!*

John J. Floto

Dear Mayor Floto:

I have been raising tropical fish for twenty years (it's my hobby), but ever since you got into City Hall my danios have been dying off. Now, just lately, the guppies are going too.

Fishwife

Dear Mrs. Fishwife:

Dr. Krementz, Assistant Freshwater Curator at the Northside Aquarium, tells me that twenty is very old for a guppy, so I do not think you should feel too much sadness or guilt about the passing of your little friends. Probably it's "all for the best," as the saying goes. As for the other possible interpretation of your brief but stimulating letter, Krementz thinks it unlikely that domestic piscine longevity is much affected by municipal politics. He adds, however, there is very little empirical data on this question. How did you vote in the last election?

J. J. F.

Hey Mr. Mayor-Man:

What's happening, baby? I guess you know this town is on a bum trip—narcs everywhere and no good weed going unpunished. Bad, *bad* scenes, man! The Acapulco up to $45 and none in sight. No Great Seedless Purple. No Tampico Taupe, no Valparaiso Violet, no Yggdrasill Yellow. Your best bread only gets a bag of stalks and pocket lint, with so many seeds you like to set your pants on fire. You trying to drive us onto the speedway, Poppa? I mean, how is a good quiet head going to get his head together?

Smokey the Bear

Dear Smokey:

Even though my opponent for this office swore that grass would grow on the streets if I were elected, possession is still a stiff rap in this state and I have to "groove" on the law. I hope you saw a recent news photograph of me in the act of destroying some two million dollars' worth of illegal marijuana, which our local agents had intercepted in a shipment of frozen instant enchiladas. On that occasion, in an impromptu address to several reporters, cameramen, and police officers gathered at the Municipal Incinerator to witness the confiscation, I stated my firm belief that each of us should be capable of attaining a state of high spirits *without recourse to artificial and illegal stimulants or narcotics.* Then, after I had lighted the blaze, our group ascended to the roof of the Incinerator Building, where I wished to inspect a defective chimney that has been giving us some trouble of late; I'm sure you know my position on clean air. More photographs were taken there while I discussed repair of the chimney (it was indeed in bad shape, emitting a heavy pall of smoke from several fissures) with our Environmental Control people. Someone then remarked on the fine view of the River and the Eutawpa Hills one is offered from the roof of the Incinerator Building, and we all concurred enthusiastically. The Deputy Incineration Engineer even stated that he had never even been *aware* of the view until that instant, which caused a hearty laugh. In the end, most of us stayed up on the roof for the rest of the afternoon and well into the evening (despite fits of coughing attributable to the faulty chimney) while we indulged in thoughtful conversations about the beauty of our old town, the nearness of the stars, the distinctly reptilian appearance of Lower Marpless Drive, etc. This pleasant interlude, in fact, caused me to be more than two hours late for the Annual Corn Planters' Ball!

I cite this incident because I think it suggests a sound policy for us all. My little homily about man's capacity for natural, self-induced euphoria seemed to strike a common chord, encouraging each of us—reporters, police officers, civic servants—to pause there on the roof and appreciate for once the simple daily wonders that surround us. I tell you, Smokey, it was *great* up there. Wow, what a view. Wow, wow!

J. J. F.

Dear Mayor Floto:

Everywhere, the erosion of comfort—nay, of mere convenience—deepens. We live up on Delancey Plains, supposedly a "good address." Lately, however, there has been a shocking decline in services, which seems to be all too typical of conditions all over our city. First the doormen vanished. Then cabs ceased to appear. Then our phone went on the fritz. Last week, no hot water. Now there's something wrong with the lights. Where are those everyday amenities that used to make city life so pleasant? What is a civilized man to do nowadays?

Old Settler

Dear Mr. Settler:

One thing a civilized man might do is go to the window and take a careful look outside, noting especially if there are any new "empty places" in the neighborhood. The entire Delancey Plains area was condemned eleven months ago, to make room for the new Frobisher International Airport, and demolition of the last buildings is scheduled to begin next Monday morning.

Let's all try a little harder to keep on our toes—O.K.?

J. J. F.

Dear Mayor Floto:

The city garbage truck that collects on our block has no American Flag on it. Our police and firemen are not afraid to show where their hearts belong, but some of these sanitation types are too stuck on themselves even to put up a little decal of Old Glory on their windshields. Maybe they'd rather make their rounds in Hanoi!

Mrs. Delight Jorgensen

Dear Mrs. Jorgensen:

Good for you! It's high time you real patriots rared up on your hind legs and showed us what you're made of. I'm sure that a person of your type will be pleased to know that your letter brought some fast results. The Character Committee of the Sanitation Workers Union launched a full investigation of the incident, and the three-man crew that used to serve your street has already been subjected to disciplinary action. Faced with undeniable evidence of flaglessness, two of these sanitation men made a full apology and confession of error; they have been permitted to remain in the Department, on a probationary basis, as apprentice manhole-flangers. The third member of the crew, however, proved to be intransigent. A thin young man with a droopy mustache, he appeared before the committee wearing tie-dyed jeans and love beads, and announced that he was joining a commune in Oregon, where he would devote himself henceforward to "cleaning out his own attic." Before turning in his badge, he played a short selection on a nose flute and then recited this piece of verse:

> ". . . in pool and rut peel parches
> Squandering ooze to squeezed dough,
>   crust, dust; stanches, starches
> Squadroned masks and manmarks
>   treadmire toil there
> Footfretted in it. Million-fuelèd,
>   nature's bonfire burns on."

The Character Committee ruled that this confusing and anarchic view of the sanitation man's profession (I am told it is a fragment of a poem by G. M. Hopkins) be stricken from the record of the hearing; it then voted its heartfelt thanks to you, Mrs. Jorgensen, for "ridding the Department of one real weirdo."

J. J. F.

Dear Mayor Floto:

I just gave up on this city. This morning the alarm went off, but instead of getting up I lay in bed awhile. I thought about getting dressed, getting my coffee, getting to the bus, riding the bus, getting off the bus and changing to the subway, going up to the office. Thought about how it looks outside these days while everybody's waiting for the bus, with the lumpy old wornout snow still there and all that's piled up on it since way back last month, and more black gock falling on it out of the sky while you're standing there, and how the air smells dead all the time now. Thought about maybe no newspaper to read because somebody's always on strike again and won't deliver the papers. Thought about shoving into the bus (and maybe the bus being late again) and me afraid I don't have the 89 cents exact fare ready and scared the bus driver will yell at me and throw me off the bus if I don't. Thought about old commuting gents in baggy coats and rubbers looking tired on the bus, and did I have a token (another 89 cents) for the subway, and then the push out of the bus and down the steps, and the cold air and dirty papers blowing up out of the subway. Then waiting down in the subway (and maybe the train being late again), and being jammed in the car with all those faces looking at you, and maybe somebody in there shouting out loud to themselves or laughing or maybe *saying* something to you because there are so many crazies around now. Thought about the train stopping in the dark tunnel and maybe getting stuck there for a while, nobody knows how long, and the crowded car all full of breathing. Then (still lying in bed) I thought, Why try? Why go to work? What's better there than here? So I stayed in bed (still here) and wrote you this letter. What's happened to our city, Mayor Floto? How did things get this way? What's going to happen to me now, for the love of God?

Patrick Mulvany

Dear Mr. Mulvany:

This has been a tough week, and your letter hasn't helped at all. This is just to tell you that I am getting tired of troublemakers like you. To be frank, I don't think you *have* a job; I think you're an unemployed writer. Do you think I can't recognize periphrasis when I see it? You and your "old commuting gents in baggy coats and rubbers looking tired on the bus"! Who do you think you are—Yeats? Jimmy Breslin?

Listen, Mulvany, I don't know how things got this way, because nobody does. The motto of this administration is something I swiped from a *real* writer, a fellow by the name of John Cage: "The truth is that everything causes everything else. We do not speak therefore of one thing causing another."

As for your last question, it might interest you to know that I read your damned letter out loud to the Board of Aldermen at our meeting this morning. We then drew the yarrow stalks (lately, we've found the "I Ching" more and more helpful in our deliberations), and what came up for you was K'un ("Oppression" or "Exhaustion"), a hexagram that includes a six at the beginning ("One sits oppressed under a bare tree and strays into a gloomy valley . . ."), a nine in the fifth place ("His nose and feet are cut off. Oppression at the hands of the man with the purple knee bands . . ."), and a six at the top ("He is oppressed by creeping vines. He moves uncertainly. . . . If one feels remorse over this and makes a start, good fortune comes"). Need I interpret? If I were you, Mulvany, I'd hop out of bed this instant and beat it out of town.

J. J. F.
(Purple Knee Bands)

Dear Mayor Floto:

What's happened to our kids? The other night I was watching the Cormorant basketball game on TV, and my son Byram, age 17, came into the room just as I am yelling something at Bingo Moussorgsky, the Cormorants' coach, who had just made another bonehead move to help the team move nearer the old cellar, and Byram laughed. "What are you laughing at?" I asked, explaining that the Cormorants were about to lose their ninth straight. "I don't care," said Byram, "and I am laughing at you." Then we "had words" and my beer got spilled on the davenport.

If our schools and churches would teach some decency and respect for parents, there wouldn't be all these demonstrations, dropouts, pornography, and trouble on the streets. And if you bleeding hearts in City Hall would spend some money to build just one Champ club for this city, instead of the losers we got now, then maybe kids would stay home with their old man once in a while and watch the game, and we wouldn't have so much immorality and crime. Right?

Big Fred

Dear Fred:

Your letter has opened my eyes. I think you're dead right, and to prove it I have just appointed Bingo Moussorgsky to fill the vacant $80,000 sinecure as our Commissioner of Housing. This may not help our slum clearance program much, but what the hell—*nothing* seems to help the slums these days, eh, Fred? This way, at least, the Cormorants will get a new coach. I think they'll need a good one, because according to information now on my desk the team is about to be subjected to a massive campaign of round-the-clock demonstrations, picketing, boycotts, sit-ins, and harangues by the Women's Liberation Front, which is charging the Cormorants with discrimination in hiring practices. How does that grab you? Don't you think that Byram will be more interested in the Cormorants when they become the first heterosexual team in the N.B.A.? Don't you think that our passionate involvement in all-male professional teams suggests a hysterical-homosexual fantasy buried deep in the American Unconscious? Why are you afraid of cellars? I suggest that you talk over all these difficult questions with your son. Everything is changing these days, Fred, believe you me.

By the way, the Moussorgsky appointment is my final one as Mayor. Your letter and most of the other citizens' letters sent me over the past six months have finally convinced me that city life, while perhaps still rewarding for some, no longer offers the same enrichment, zest, and challenge to high accomplishment that it once did for me. Or, as Mrs. Floto put it the other day, "Who wants to be Chief Kook in Kooksville?" By the time you read this, we will already be in residence, along with the children, in a somewhat smaller settlement out in Oregon, where I plan to undertake a regimen of fasting and meditation at the feet of an erstwhile young colleague of mine who also recently retired from the *faubourgs*. Please let me know how the Cormorants make out. Or don't—see if I care.

John J. Floto

Over My Head

(The Plimpton Factor Invades American Letters)

My agent, Morrie, came to see me in the clubhouse after a night game in May. I was surprised to see him; he hadn't done any business for me all season. Last year, it was different. After I'd hung up that good E.R.A., third best in the league, and pitched three shutout innings in the All-Star game, I was a hot item, and Morrie kept me busy. I did comedy bits for Vitalis and Supphose, made guest shots with Carson and Griffin, appeared on panels to talk about juvenile delinquency and air pollution and missile deployment, and all that stuff. It was a groove. But this spring I was a holdout for five weeks, and I never did get trained right. I had this sore arm all through April. Then I got bombed out in Oakland and Kansas City on the same swing west, and I lost my spot in the rotation. It got so I'd been picking up the paper every day to see if I'd been traded to Montreal. So why would Morrie want to see me?

"Buzzie, bay-bee!" Morrie said. "How's the arm?"

"It fell off last week," I said. "I'm having it embalmed."

"How'd you like to make a wad of cash?" he asked.

"Doing what—selling birdseed door to door?"

"No, Buzz. It's a special deal, something brand-new. There's a couple of thousand clams in it for you. Listen, you ever read that magazine *Sports Illusory*?"

"Are you *kidding*?"

"Let me put it another way," Morrie said. "Did you read that book by the writer who pitched against an all-star bigleague team in an exhibition game? That society cat, George

Plimpton? You know his thing. Like he hadn't pitched since school, and he wanted to see what it would feel like out there throwing to Willie Mays and all them, and then write about it. He put it all in a book, his first book. It's called *Out of My League*."

"I know about it, but I haven't read it," I said. "It's even in paperback. I've been meaning to get it. Marianne Moore gave it a terrific plug, I think in the *New York Review of Books*." I was getting interested.

"O.K.," Morrie said. "Now, here's the MacGuffin. *Sports Illusory* wants you to do the same thing, almost. They want you to spend a day working on the staff of a magazine, just like a big-time writer or editor. Then you write a piece about it for them. You dig? It's a hell of a switch, and it backs up their big theme that ballplayers are funky, high-type Joes, interested in the arts and all, just like their average readers. They'll pay two big rocks for the job. How does it hit you?"

"Well. . . ." I said. I tried to sound dubious, but the truth is my heart was racing with excitement. It was crazy and it would take nerve, but what big-leaguer could turn down a chance like this? Like every red-blooded American ballplayer, I've always wanted to be a writer. I've read every word Norman Mailer has written for *Life*. I never miss Gore Vidal or Bill Buckley on the tube. And plenty of ballplayers have made it in the world of letters, haven't they? Look at Jim Bouton. Look at Eugene McCarthy. Way back in my sandlot days, I knew all about Jim Brosnan, the Cincinnati pitcher who wrote those books. I even copied some of his mannerisms—the way he muttered those lines from Pound and Eliot when he glared down at the batters. "What's the magazine I'd be working for?" I managed to ask.

"It's the best, Buzz," he said. "The *Dijon Review*."

"Wow!" I murmured. This *was* the big league! The *Dijon Review*—the most intellectual, the most shrill, the most insufferable of the little reviews! I could feel the sweat beginning to trickle down my wrists, and I knew I'd lose my nerve if I thought about it a minute longer. "O.K.," I said, looking up at Morrie and trying to manage a smile, "I'll do it."

The day set for my adventure was a Monday in June, an open date on the team's schedule, and the intervening weeks flew by all too fast for my heightened state of nerves. More than once, I picked up the telephone to call Morrie and tell him I had thought better of the whole foolhardy scheme, but some curious sense of pride always made me put it down again. After all, I'd remind myself, I was introspective, well read, full of normal literary ambitions. Even if I got my ears knocked off, it would be something to tell my grandchildren about—the day I matched my taste against the best aesthetes of my time. I found it hard to concentrate on my work; sitting in the bullpen during a Sunday doubleheader, I would lose track of the score. The roar of the crowd and the harsh cries of the peanut vendors would fade from my ears, replaced in my mind by the crisp crackle of manuscripts, the sibilant crawl of blue pencils across paper, and the civilized murmur of epigrams and barbed rejoinders. Once, in New York, I slipped out of my room at five in the morning and walked through the dawn-swept streets and found myself at last standing in front of the West Side brownstone that houses the editorial offices of the *Dijon Review*. "In there," I whispered to myself, eying the temple, "just a few days from now. . . ." Inside my pockets, my typing fingers were tapping out unconscious arpeggios.

In the last few days, the realities of plans and training helped to steady me. I went all over town to costume myself correctly— striped bells and fringed Custer tunic from the East Village, granny shades from Meyrowitz, Gucci loafers. I bought a black shirt at a police outfitter's on Spring Street and then, in an act of pure braggadocio, completed the getup with a white snap-brim Bogey hat from Tripler. Out of sight! One day, when I arrived thus attired at the ballpark, Clancy, the manager, stopped me with a puzzled look on his big face. "You got a shoulder kink, Buzz?" he asked. "You're walking kinda crooked. Maybe you need an hour in the whirlpool bath, hunh?"

I blushed and straightened up, assuring him I was all right. But I knew what had happened. My old Capote crouch, the one I affected so assiduously in my youth, had come back upon me. A good omen indeed!

Friday night before my Monday, Buck Willis, my roomie, and I drove up to Yaddo. It was after ten when we arrived, however, and a surly gatekeeper barred our way. "All the typewriters is locked up for the night," he muttered. "All the writers, too. Besides, I can't go around letting just any old hack in here." Disappointed, we saved something from the journey by circling through Bread Loaf, where a kindly lady who teaches Middle English at Mount Holyoke allowed me to loosen up on her big Remington. I worked out for an hour, testing old muscles. My motion was good, but I wasn't hitting the space bar with the old confidence.

I was ready when Monday morning came. I arose feeling refreshed, aware of a faint tremor in the backs of my knees, but grateful, on the whole, that *der Tag* had arrived. Then, as I stood in front of my mirror, making last adjustments to my uniform, my heart gave a great leap of dismay. I had no Fowler! It was a shocking oversight on my part. I could not turn up at the *Dijon Review* and confess to such an omission, and I was only too aware that no editor willingly lends his Fowler, even to an officemate who is trying to break out of a slump. That is one of the oldest superstitions in the game. I grabbed the telephone and called Lefty Kolb, our team's affable knuckle-baller. "Listen, Lefty," I said, spilling out the words in my haste, "have you got an old Fowler you could lend me for the day?"

"A what?" he said sleepily.

"A Fowler's *Modern English Usage*. Any edition will do, but I've got to have it right away."

"Gee, no, Buzz," he said. "I happen to know, because I was looking for mine only last week. I'm sorry as hell."

I thanked him, hung up, and hurried out to see if I could buy the volume. But no bookstores were open at that early hour. I had to settle for a Little Golden Dictionary, purchased from a drugstore. I carried it under my arm all day, hoping my temporary colleagues would accept it as a personal literary eccentricity.

"Editors' entrance?" I inquired, standing outside an open door in the dim third-floor corridor. I could feel my heart thumping under my buckskins.

"It's the only door we got," said the young man sitting inside, not lifting his eyes from his *Daily News*.

I entered, removed my hat, and extended my hand. "Ty Cobb," I said, employing the amusing sobriquet we had agreed upon at *Sports Illusory*. "I'm sort of working here today."

"I heard," the man said, giving me a soft, dry handshake. "I'm Eric." He had a skimpy mustache under an enormous haystack of unkempt blond hair, and I noticed that he wore purple socks and a pair of cracked patent-leather pumps.

The room was littered with newspapers, disorderly piles of letters—bills, by the look of them—and empty cardboard containers of coffee. There was a standing screen to my left, and from behind this I heard the low hum of voices and the clink of teacups in the next room. These scholarly sights and sounds unmanned me for a moment. "Look," I said to Eric. "Can I warm with you for a few minutes? Before I go in there?"

"O.K.," he said indifferently. "But I'm just the office boy around here."

We warmed for ten minutes, tossing aphorisms and capping easy quotations. I began to feel better, and I ventured a pitch I had used with some success in college. "Isn't it curious," I said, "that neither Cowley nor Trilling has observed that the water images in the final sentences of both *A Farewell to Arms* and *Tender Is the Night* are direct, if unconscious, inheritors of a lineage tracing back to the closing passages of *Moby Dick,* in which the *Pequod* slips beneath those tiresomely symbolic waves? It's a curious lacuna in our critical thesaurus."

The effect of this upon Eric was unexpected. He straightened up and glared at me angrily. "Watch that stuff," he said bitterly.

"No rhetorical questions without you give me a warning, see? Watch that showboating, buster."

"Oh, sure," I said, abashed. "Sure, sure, sure. I'm sorry. Anything you say."

I was now ready; the hour had come. Eric led me into the back room, and I introduced myself awkwardly. I recognized most of the faces, of course; as a boy, I had pasted their likenesses, clipped from Sunday book-review sections, inside my locker door. Blevins Carroll, the editor, was seated at a high old-fashioned roll-top desk, his great forehead gleaming palely above a green eyeshade. Morgan MacPhee and Hastings Latrobe, the devastating, heavily bearded pair recently purchased from *Partisan Review* in exchange for five British critics and an undisclosed amount of cash, were bent over the morning *Times*, working the crossword puzzle together. A fourth figure was stretched out on an old cot against one wall, his head buried in his arms. From time to time, he groaned. Too much *espresso* the night before, I guessed privately. The first three acknowledged my presence with curt nods. I was aware of a professionalism, a truly burning intolerance, in this room, and I knew happily that I would not encounter any false bonhomie here today. These men were admitting me to their company as an equal, with all the cynical hostility of the élite.

Thus encouraged, I began to take careful note of details— material to flesh out my narrative for *Sports Illusory*. I perceived that although Blevins Carroll talked out of the right side of his mouth, he wrote with his left hand, a tremendous defensive advantage in an editor who is also a novelist. (Most editors are right-handed.) Like all true intellectuals, these men smoked cigarettes. There were open packs all over the room, in pockets and on desks, within reach of limber, preoccupied fingers. Intellectuals light their cigarettes with matches, never lighters, striking flame with a single, deft inward motion, and usually throwing the used match stubs on the floor. I noted that the members of the staff usually addressed each other by their first names, only rarely employing such alternatives as "old chap" or "fella." This fact, in turn, led me to a further discovery: many critics have first names that are more customarily surnames—Blevins, Morgan, Hastings, and so forth. This gives them a superiority in bylines almost from birth.

"Well, we might as well get to it," Carroll said at last. He leaned forward and tossed me a thick, untidy sheaf of manuscript. "Anything here we should use?" he asked.

I licked my lips. I was aware that the three were watching me closely. I looked down at the manuscript. It had been scrawled, apparently with a blunt pencil, on flimsy sheets of pink paper. It was in a language I didn't recognize, but the varying length of the lines made me guess it was a piece of free verse. "Hmmm," I said, stalling. "Well . . . Well, it isn't typewritten."

The three men looked at each other in surprise, exchanging smiles of apparent relief. "Yes," Latrobe said eagerly, "and we don't accept untyped submissions."

"I never thought of that!" MacPhee said.

"And he didn't enclose any return postage," Carroll added. He took the manuscript from me and dropped it in a wastebasket. "Nice work, Mr. Cobb," he said, looking at me with new respect.

Alas, it was not to remain as easy as that. Overconfident, working too fast, I soon found myself making the simplest anti-intellectual blunders. I voted against a film review, a reevaluation of Bugs Bunny as the American *Übermensch,* on the ground that it was frivolous. Carroll snatched it back angrily, stating that it would probably be the lead article in their next issue. "Don't you know Warner Brothers cartoons are way, way in, man?" he said. Then I voted *for* an essay on the nursery years of Samuel Beckett, which struck me as fresh and amusing. "Pap!" Carroll snorted. "*Kitschy*-koo," Latrobe muttered. The figure on the couch shuddered at my obtuseness. A terrible exhaustion flowed over me. I was in deep waters, far over my head.

At this juncture, Eric's face appeared around the side of the screen. "Omnescu is here for his interview," he announced.

For a moment, my nerve failed me utterly. Tired, flustered, my ill-conditioned critical reflexes already screaming in protest,

I was now to face the most feared literary slugger of our time. Omnescu, the free-swing Rumanian avant-gardist, author of three volumes of *haiku* written in classical Etruscan, was about to take part in one of the *Dijon Review*'s famed interviews-in-depth, and *I* was expected to lead our team's assault. "No, no!" I cried weakly. "It's too much to ask. I can't go on. These bone chips in my writing hand . . ."

"Courage, Cobb," Latrobe whispered in my ear. "We'll be here behind you, fielding the answers. Just lay your searching questions down the middle."

Well, I tried. I'll say that for myself in retrospect. When the great man had been ushered in and seated in a broken armchair, I cleared my throat and forced myself to look at his fearsome visage rising above his filthy turtleneck sweater and huge shoulders like an angry winter moon over a range of mountains. His cold zircon eyes, which I had seen heretofore only from a seat in the back rows of the Y.M.H.A. Poetry Center auditorium, now fixed themselves on me with horrid anticipation. I thought confusedly of my success with the foreign manuscript, and stammered out, "Mr. Omnescu, do you, uh, write with a p-pencil?"

To my astonishment, he popped a soft answer straight back to my teammates. "Hah!" he said. "Axcellant qvastion. Axcellant! Until last year, Omnescu writes always with pancil. But last January, with Guggenheim money, Omnescu buys electric typewriter. Results: electric!" And for the next ten minutes he chatted warmly about his rapport with a writing device so happily symbolic of our depersonalized milieu, while the editors scribbled busily and gratefully in their notebooks.

Unfortunately, I was now so emboldened that I decided on another change-up pitch. It was to be my last effort of the day. "Sir," I said, "have you read and been influenced by Yogi Berra's autobiography?"

His face turned, red, then purple. "Yoga!" he exploded. "You ask me—Omnescu—about yoga? That qvackery? You vaste my time with meesticism, with Indian gymnastics for housewives on nut diets? Omnescu will put you straight on yoga, you meeserable counter-intellactual." Spluttering, jabbering incoherently, laps-

ing frequently into his native tongue, he launched on a mono-
logue so verbose and so rambling that long before he had
finished, Carroll and MacPhee and Latrobe had dropped their
pencils out of sheer ennui.

"That'll be all," Carroll said to me crisply. He beckoned to
Eric to take my place in the circle of chairs. I had been relieved
again. I was washed up in this league.

Weeping, I dropped my Little Golden Dictionary and stum-
bled out and down the stairs toward the street. I had forgotten
my Bogey hat, but I knew I would never need it again. Dejected,
sore of head and spirit, I trudged slowly toward the subway.
Then, just before I reached the corner, my glance fell upon two
ragged urchins in my path. They were bent over, unaware of
me, writing busily with chalk on the pavement. Their scrawled
words stretched the entire width of the sidewalk, from curb to
building front.

"Hey, Jim-mee!" one of them yelled. "Watch me, Jim-mee!
Watch me write. I'm William Styron, Jim-mee! I'm Styron writing!"

"Go-wann!" the other called back, scribbling excitedly. "Lookit
me, Billy. Watch *me* write! *I'm* Elizabeth Hardwick!"

Touched, deeply moved by these innocent gamins, I blew my
nose and began to cheer up. "The game will go on," I whispered
to myself. "Even without me, it will go on. The great American
pastime will never die."

More Film Fun

(Tentative Program Notes for Another Week of High
Cinematic Entertainment, Drawn Up After a Study
of the Festival News from Lincoln Center)

The Peapod Bowl (*Atafumu*)

In a dazzling, deeply significant switch from the decadent opu-
lence that marked his *Deacon Watanabe and the Shower Clogs* and
the rustic crudity of his *The Rice Splitter* (winner of the Grand
Prix at the McKeesport Fesitval), Protubo Mitihara has gone to
the contemporary half-world of the Osaka bowling alleys to bring
us a disquieting, understated, and unlovely tale of a teen-age
pinspotter who is suffering from a crisis of identity brought on
by the threat of automation. The symbolism here (the round
perfection of the bowling balls marred by ugly yet necessary
finger holes) is pervasive yet never blatant. Henry Mancini has
composed a brilliant score that combines the harsh thunder of
falling tenpins with the classic tinkling dissonances of Japanese
folk opera. You will especially remember the painful eleven-
minute sequence, played in total silence and darkness, in which
Zenzu Fumita, in the role of the hero's uncle, gropes for the
light switch in the men's room.

Paddle Your Own Canoe (*Pas de le Rhône que Nous*)

It was inevitable, given the long Gallic fascination with *Le Far
Ouest,* that Jean-Paul Luc would eventually fashion a film out of
Cooper's *Leatherstocking Tales,* but who would have guessed that
his freehand cinematic translation would transform Chingach-

gook into a middle-aged, sexually repressed Michelin restaurant scout (Jean-Paul Poulenc), or that Natty Bumppo would emerge as Natalie Beaupré, a shy yet smoldering Girl Scout leader (Jeanne-Paule Morbideau) who loses first her compass and then her virginity during a hike in the Bois de Boulogne? This film, frankly prurient, never escapes into easy sentimentalism, and though some in the audience may be shocked by the filling-station scene or the episode of the *marrons glacés,* none will deny that Luc's cinematographic intelligence has brought us a fresh comprehension of the "innocence" of the great American woods.

Nibbles

The National Film Board of Canada, which has been responsible for some of the best documentaries in recent years (its vivid *Hockey Puck Injuries* won second prize at the Ottawa Biennale), has surpassed itself with this unflinching study of nail-biting habits in a typical middle-income household. Although Director Tony Garwood and Producer Al Gurtch stick manfully to their subject while depicting, with brisk crosscutting, the slow decline of parental confidence suffered by teen-agers with low cuticle resistance, the real hero of the film is downtown Saskatoon, a *mise en scène* of surprising beauty and ambivalence. This masterpiece proves again that subject matter is no obstacle, and almost of no concern, to modern cinematic genius.

The Groans of Winter (*Vintersgrönen*)

This rare print of Gunnar Malmstrom's much-whispered-about early chef-d'œuvre offers a first chance for American audiences to see an uncut version of a film from the Swedish master's pre-religious period. The movie, which has been banned for more than a decade in Spain and Jersey City, deals with the progressive alienation, aberration, and madness of a young Stockholm eel-sorter after he surprises his mother and his aged tutor together in a sauna bath. Shot mainly with a handheld and defective 16-mm camera, it contains crude, juvenile versions of Malmstrom's purposefully "tiresome" repeated symbols, juxtapositions, and allegorical leitmotivs, and as such is of inestimable cinematohistorical value. And, as Henry Miller has said, "This film is not *just* about lust and insanity. It is also a wet fish in the face to all those who would deny the delicacy of the human spirit."

Once Again Chapatties (*Chapatty, Chapatty, Chapatty*)

Has Indian farce been done to death? Certainly not! Once again the puckish Ram Mukerjee has dug deep into his inexhaustible bag of cinematic magic tricks and wry ironies to bring us this heartwarming tragicomedy about a Hindu family struggling to find its multiple identity against the age-old handicaps of illiteracy, matriarchy, monkey worship, and boredom. On the surface, this leisurely, 210-minute epic merely recounts the effects of a crippling strike at the local paraldehyde works upon a small north-Indian mud village, but woven through this coarse fabric are bright threads of allegory and impudence that ask profound questions about the direction and meaningfulness of our Western agrarian policies. On the same bill, there will be a fifty-minute short that depicts, with utter frankness and in fantastic colors, the sinuous dalliance and courtship habits of the oarfishes of the Great Barrier Reef; the musical accompaniment, singularly apt, is by the Vienna Boys' Choir.

Little Men

At last, the public will have an opportunity to make up its own mind about the merits of this filmic *cause célèbre!* Does this eleven-minute, 8-mm entry constitute "an exceptionally faithful, heartbreaking, and utterly poetic rendering of the ancient myth of Bellerophon and Pegasus," as it has been characterized by film historian and curator Fermin Terwilliger, who accidentally came upon a print in the back room of a rare book and film emporium on Sixth Avenue? Or is it, in the words of its surprised creator, Sergei (Blue Serge) Eisenstein, "Just another piece of schlocky beefcake"? Mr. Eisenstein, whose other credits include *Mondo*

Hondo, A Streetcar Named David, and *The Wedding of the Member,* also disclaims any connection between the well-known Louisa May Alcott novel and his own classic of the same name, which depicts with utter frankness a startling simultaneous search for identity by three jockeys in the steam-room of a West Coast Y.M.C.A.

The Mars Wheel

The only other American entry in this festival is of the new, hard-line, super-realistic Hollywood genre, as insistent and electrifying as a Dexedrine tablet. This drama, set in the America of the day after tomorrow, deals with a frightening power struggle that ensues when the paranoid top magnate of a vast car-rental agency attempts to seize control of the National Aeronautics and Space Administration, thus blackmailing Congress into a repeal of the corporate income-tax statutes. The gripping climax, all the more convincing for its unlikelihood, comes when the C.I.A. must track down the Chief Executive's purloined credit card in time to abort a doomed billion-dollar Mars shot. Omar Sharif easily "steals" the acting honors with his bijou portrayal of the Minority Whip.

Oogu (*Oogu*)

Even the most dedicated film enthusiast might hesitate at the prospect of sitting through a three-hour movie that deals with an eighty-five-year-old Eskimo grandmother who suffers from psychopathic fear of the cold and who is exiled, toothless, to the Husky pens after a lifetime of honorable boot-chewing. But doubters will think twice when they learn that this haunting, blizzard-swept drama comes from the hand of Luigi DaRimini, creator of the triumphant, lusty *Saltimbocca* (winner of the Prix-Fixe at the Pomfret School Festival). DaRimini's patient, unwinking camera and an untranslated, undubbed sound track that is alive with Eskimo gutterals and canine snarls combine, however slowly, to bring alive a relationship between the old woman, the lead dog, and a herd of unseen caribou, that is pure Genet. Klikiat Ipaka, the aged heroine, establishes herself in this, her first film, as an actress of impenetrable subtlety. Not to be missed!

Shorts Unlimited!

Almost everybody is making films these days, and this closing day's program is a potpourri of shorter recent works that illustrates the unlimited new horizons of the medium. Among the forty-seven featurettes are *The Trial, Conviction, and Execution of Chicken-Licken,* a film conceived, acted, directed, and shot in its entirety by Miss Hyssop's second graders' workshop in Azuza, California; and *Innies and Outies,* a sensitive nature study produced by the Florida Navel-Orange Growers Co-op. In an altogether different vein is *O Quel Cruller!*—at first glance a rather far-fetched nudie farce, which turns out to be a clever new rendering of the annual stockholders' report of the Rappaport Bagel & Doughnut Corp. Here too is *Amoebophrenia,* a short combining microphotography and cartoon doodling (a process developed by the Rockefeller Institute Film Workshop), which explicates, with wacky interpolated dialogue, the loss of identity sensed by an amoeba as it undergoes binary fission. Finally, mention must be made of Anders Mickoszy's *Bottle Fatigue* (winner of the Silver Potato at the Boise Festival), a stunningly arrayed montage of abandoned bedsprings, old bus tokens, and broken glass, which says more about the slow poison of prejudice and the new strides being made by group therapy than a dozen weighty books of sociology! The utter silence in the audience during the running of this two-reeler and the relieved applause at its termination are a tribute to its high seriousness—and to the maturity of the cinema art in our time.

Turtletaub and
the Foul Distemper

The facts concerning last winter's mystifying New England airplane accident—referred to variously in the press as the "Vanishing Pilot Case" or the "Pancaked Jetliner Puzzle"—are so fresh in the public mind that I hesitate to reopen the matter, lest I be found guilty of second-hand sensationalism. Yet the truth, or as much of it as perhaps we will ever know, deserves to be set forth, if only because it forms part of a far darker and more tangled tale that certain authorities wish to suppress. Foremost among these is my old friend Inspector Turtletaub, of the Special Assignments Bureau, who first told me the whole story and yet who now claims concern for my health and whimpers that "the world is not ready" for the terrible truth. Lies, lies! My health has never been better—ha, ha!—and here, sipping champagne high above the Atlantic as I fly eastward to a new life, I pick up my pen and prepare to set down nothing less than a true history. I defy you, Lionel Turtletaub, to deny a syllable of it!

The details of the accident are easily set forth in précis. On a stormy March afternoon, a regularly scheduled airliner bound for Boston radioed the Logan tower to report a sudden failure of all navigational and directional instruments, as well as an undiagnosed and uncorrectable loss of power. The plane, in short, was lost and on the point of making a forced landing. This was the last radio contact. At 5:07 P.M. (E.S.T.), the inhabitants of Burbage Fens, Mass., a small village near Athol, heard the noise of a plane circling in low-lying clouds directly overhead—a roar that was abruptly silenced as the plane seemed to go into the ground in the environs of the Presumptionist Brothers monastery on a hillside just north of town. Hurrying there, the alarmed villagers were relieved to find the plane not only intact but entirely undamaged. The pilot, it could be seen, had made a brilliant wheels-up landing on the lawn of the monastery, formerly a large private estate. The monks, who had been at table in their refectory, were now trying to pry open the airliner's cabin doors. When they did so, they found the fifty-three passengers, the co-pilot, the engineer, and three stewardesses still strapped in their seats. None, it was quickly determined, had suffered so much as a bump or a scratch, yet all fifty-eight of them were semiconscious. Moaning and shuddering, sometimes crying out in evident horror, they were quickly removed to a nearby hospital, where they were found to be suffering from shock. Recovery was rapid, and within twenty-four hours all of the survivors were released. To this day, however, not one of them has ventured a word of explanation as to the circumstances of the crash; if pressed by relatives or reporters, they grow pale, tremble uncontrollably, and make piteous attempts to leave the room. The findings of the National Transportation Safety Board have never been released. Nor has any information been given as to the whereabouts of the pilot, Captain Sebastian Moran, or of one of the monks, a novice known as Brother Larry, neither of whom has been seen since the moment of the crash.

There, as far as the public knows, the matter stands—just where it stood that evening six weeks ago when Inspector Turtletaub finished his press briefing and the last reporters, still muttering their complaints and questions, had been led from his office. The last, that is, save I. Turtletaub looked up from his desk and saw me still in my accustomed chair.

"Didn't you hear me, Humberstone?" he growled. "That's all. There's the door."

"I heard you, Lionel," I said. I walked over to the door and snapped the lock. Then I threw my pencils and copy-paper into the wastebasket. Then I held open my jacket for his inspection. "No visitors, no notes, no tapes," I said. "Now, Lionel, off the record. . . ."

He rose and passed his hands nervously over his towering

forehead. "I'd like to, Humberstone," he said unhappily. "But this, believe me, is a case like no other. It must remain forever veiled."

"Lionel," I said reproachfully. "This is me, Walt Humberstone—or rather, I. Have I ever violated a confidence?"

"You don't *understand!*" he burst out. "It's you I must protect, along with everybody else. Everyone out there!" He made a sweeping gesture with one hand. "They're not strong enough—*nobody* is strong enough to hear this!"

I smiled. "Remember the Shopworn Torso case?" I said. "Remember the Hoboken Glutton? I helped you with those, Lionel. I'm a tough old newshawk, so leave my feelings out of this. You've been on this case for weeks now, and I can see what it's doing to you. What was it—a new kind of hijack? Nerve gas, maybe? Weathermen? When will you make a collar?"

He shook his head again, threw himself into his chair, and then jumped up and resumed pacing. "No arrests, no arrests," he muttered to himself. "They're gone. Two twisted minds like that, once again loosed on the world. . . . Who would believe it?"

"*I'd* believe it, Lionel," I said gently.

"Very well!" he cried, once more flinging himself behind his desk. "But remember—you begged me. Don't blame me later!" He took a bunch of keys from his side pocket, unlocked a drawer in his desk, and drew forth a bulging file.

"You said 'two twisted minds,' " I said, "Do you mean that the pilot and the monk were in it together?"

"Yes, of course," Turtletaub said, ruffling papers.

"But the monk was on the ground."

"Exactly. The co-pilot's evidence was perfectly clear about that. Seventeen passengers on the right-hand side of the plane confirmed his report. As the plane slithered across the lawn on its belly, the monk, later said to be 'Brother Larry,' ran forward from under a tree and seemed to be struck down by the right wingtip. They could all see him lying there as the plane stopped."

"But that sounds as if the monk was—" I began.

"Was *waiting* for the plane, yes," the Inspector said excitedly. "Was 'in it' with the pilot, yes. Was a joint planner and principal in a plot of truly diabolical premeditation! Was a criminal impostor of monstrous patience and cunning! Was, in short, a match for his partner in evil, the rascally Captain 'Sebastian Moran.' Ah, my friend, the arrogance of that name! The deranged brilliance of it!" He broke off and shook a sheaf of papers in my face. "They are the same pair!" he said fiercely. "The pattern is all too clear. Brother Larry is the North Woods Barrymore, and Captain Moran is the Mad Editor. They have struck again!"

"What?" I cried, utterly dumbfounded now. "Who? When? Where?"

Inspector Turtletaub looked at me musingly. "Where shall we begin, Humberstone?" he said. "These are very deep waters."

He began, a few minutes later, with the Moses Paulding disappearance. I remembered the story—a minor mystery of a decade before. Moses Paulding, a respectable advertising account executive, had vanished after a cocktail party in Darien, where he lived. There had been a fracas of some kind. Paulding had walked out, never to be seen again.

"Moses Paulding," Turtletaub told me, "was suffering from Retardate Wildeanism, which means that he was never able to think of clever remarks until too late, usually the next morning. This is a commonplace ailment—we all have it to some degree—but Paulding's was a bad case. He was known in Darien as something of a dullard, yet at home in bed at night or while shaving the next morning, he would suddenly burst out laughing as he thought of some flashing riposte, some edged apothegm, to throw into a conversation already hours or days dead. One day while driving in his car alone, he thought of a bon mot concerning Angela Thirkell, the English novelist, and was so convulsed that he had to pull over to the median strip to compose himself. That evening, he told his wife the joke—she filled me in on all this, much later—and explained to her that he had resolved to remember this one until it was needed. He planted it in his memory, so that he would be able to pluck it forth, casually and elegantly, at the very first mention of Angela Thirkell at somebody's dinner table or poolside party. The trouble was, of course, that Angela Thirkell wasn't exactly the best-known author in Darien. Oh, one may suppose that a few of his neighbors had heard of her or read her, but it wasn't a name that came up every day."

"Still isn't," I said, yawning.

"Very well," Turtletaub said, eying me. "*Bref,* nobody mentioned Angela Thirkell. There was our friend Paulding preparing his one little firecracker before every dinner party and sociable—fondling and polishing it in his pocket, so to speak—and no one would light the fuse. Five years went by, and no Thirkell. She even died in that time, but no one in Darien noticed it or mentioned the fact in front of Paulding. The poor fellow was going mad. He'd almost forgotten, and then, kismet!—he was a guest at a large summer lawn party when suddenly he thought he heard the magic sound of 'Angela Thirkell' drift through the evening air. The voice he'd heard was at the opposite end of a ninety-seven-foot veranda, but Paulding dropped his drink, left the people he was with, and ran all the way over there, shoving through the other guests and upsetting a tray of sandwiches on the way. When he got there, it turned out to be a group of visitors who were total strangers to him—and the name they had dropped, by the way, was Studs Terkel, not Angela Thirkell—but Paulding pushed his way right in among them, and then, still panting but trying to appear offhand and debonair, he said, 'Well, *I've* always thought Angela Thirkell was a thquare.' "

"What!" I said, sitting up in my chair.

"That's what *they* said," said the Inspector. "They made him repeat it, the poor, doomed soul, and this time the whole party, easily sixty or seventy people, was listening, and nobody laughed. Nobody said a word, in fact. And at that instant, we may safely speculate, the mind of Moses Paulding cracked apart, like a dropped fingerbowl. He walked slowly down the veranda steps and up the slate path to the driveway, and then turned and faced them. He lifted both his arms, and in a hair-raising, keening voice he cried, 'Revenge shall be miii-nnne!' He left, and no one has seen him—at least, under *that* name—to this day."

"Serves him right," I said, rubbing my burning temples. "But what about the plane? What about—"

Turtletaub held up his hand, consulted another file, poured himself a sip of water from his decanter, and resumed. "Time: seven years ago," he said. "Place: a certain village in northern-most Quebec, well above Chicoutimi. The only inhabitants are trappers and lumberjacks, with the exception of the monks res-ident in a large local monastery. The only newspaper—"

"*Another* monastery?" I said.

"You've the makings of a detective, my good fellow," said the Inspector. "Yes. And the only newspaper is a modest bilingual weekly called *L'Éclaireur du Muskeg.* Properly modest, because there is normally no news whatsoever in this godforsaken com-pound—no arrivals, no departures, few females, few diversions. The only excitement, in fact, is the annual stage presentation performed by the inhabitants of the monastery. This play is a regionally famous institution—or has been ever since its man-agement was put entirely into the hands of a monk named—" He paused and consulted his notes. "Yes. Father Marcel Squegg."

"Funny name," I said.

"No," said Turtletaub grimly. "Not funny in the least. Well, Squegg, we have learned, was a first-class theatrical director and actor, an enthusiastic *metteur en scène* who succeeded in involving every one of his fellow ecclesiastics in the annual mumming. There was a different presentation each autumn—one year a farce, the next a musical, the next Shakespeare, and so forth. Whatever its nature, Squegg directed, handled the casting and lighting, and played the leading role. He was brilliant, and his foremost supporter and press agent was the local newspaper, which, curiously enough, was also written and edited and printed entirely by one man, a friend of Squegg's."

"The Mad Editor!" I whispered. "And the North Woods Bar-rymore!"

"Exactly. Thus the editor dubbed him in the newspaper after

Squegg's *succès fou* as Hamlet one year. He gave the monk the entire front page—photographs, headlines, and the better part of the rave notice. Unsurprisingly, such news quickly spread across the province, and soon word—the expected word—came up from the diocese, which permitted Squegg to put into motion the final details of the plan. He was summoned in by the abbot and reminded of the sin of pride. He was ordered to continue as director of forthcoming plays but was enjoined from further stardom. Squegg, of course, consented to abase himself. Well, the next year's item of repertory was a full-scale revival of *Uncle Tom's Cabin,* and the customary sellout complement of woodsy first-nighters turned out to cheer their local Garrick—only to find his name absent from the bill. Squegg was in the play, in fact, but was not noticed, for he had cast himself as one of the dogs that follow Eliza across the ice in the melodramatic chase scene. He was completely encased in a bloodhound costume and was not recognized when he went sniffing and baying across the stage."

"I hope the play was better than this story," I said irritably. "This is the stupidest—"

"We'll see who's stupid!" Turtletaub snapped. "You are now in precisely the same position as those poor, helpless reubens. The Mad Editor and that fiendish priest have you at their mercy, and you don't even know it." He extracted a faded newspaper clipping from his file. "Here is the story about *Uncle Tom's Cabin* that appeared in the *Éclaireur* the next morning. Never mind the review—just read the headline."

It was a banner right across the top of the page, and I read it out loud: " 'PÈRE SQUEGG IN HOUND RÔLE.' "

Turtletaub stooped and retrieved the clipping, which had fluttered from my fingers. I was at his desk, emptying the decanter over my head.

"The newspaper office was sacked that same morning," he went on. "The townspeople tore the place apart. By that time, of course, Paulding and the priest had long since departed, having made good their departure under cover of darkness. Paulding, we now know, was the editor. They were in it together, right from the start. We don't know where they met, of course, but we do know who Squegg was and how he got that way."

"No!" I spluttered. "*Please,* no. I don't want to hear about it. Nix."

Inexorably, he reached for another file and went on. "Originally, a Father Martin Quist, an unremarkable young priest in a poor Midwest parish," he intoned. "So poor, in fact, that they had to let out some of the rooms in the rectory to boarders, in order to make ends meet. Well, this was well back in the fifties, in the unlamented McCarthy era, and soon ugly stories were afloat to the effect that one of the boarders was a Communist and possibly an atheist. Parish morale declined and suspicions were rife, and one Sunday Father Quist determined to put an end to the matter. He arose in the pulpit after Mass—"

I put my hands up, as if to ward off a blow.

"—and told the congregation that there was nothing in it. The accused boarder, he said, was not a Catholic, but he certainly wasn't a Communist or an atheist. 'In fact,' he told them, holding back a smile, 'I can assure you that we have nothing here but an unconfirmed roomer.' " Turtletaub flicked me a glance. "Maybe I should spell that out for you," he said. "He meant—"

"I *know* what he meant!" I said, gagging. "A man like that— Why, I would have—Excommunication!"

"Not quite," said the Inspector, "but he was out of office and out of the parish by nightfall. Exile and Squeggdom ensued. Before he left town, you see, he, too, made a public vow of revenge. Exactly like Paulding."

"Which brings your story full circle," I said, rising hastily and grabbing for my raincoat. "And a terrible story it's been, too. Well, thanks, Lionel, and—"

"*Sit down!*" Turtletaub thundered. "We haven't even come to the plane crash yet. And you asked for this—remember?"

The next hour dragged by painfully as the Inspector described his own involvement in the case—the urgent request for his services, first from the Canadian Mounties, then by Interpol;

the months of careful backtracking and painstaking police work that uncovered the identities of the two lunatics; and the fears, kept very secret, of forensic medical experts that the Paulding-Quist syndrome might prove in some way to be contagious, thus threatening the Western mind with a truly terrifying new madness. These fears, in fact, were deepened by the number of parallel cases that distracted Turtletaub from his manhunt. There were indeed other victims of the foul distemper, and Turtletaub, in his methodical manner, spared me none of the details.

"Now, you take the Lord Tweedy business, back in '65," he said. "That certainly *sounded* like Paulding's work. A shocking tale. A wealthy British tourist had arrived in a little Alpine village one afternoon, where he joined a crowd of local citizens watching a burning chalet. Could he have *lit* that fire? Possibly. We shall never know. As the flames died down, he observed quietly that it was rather early in the season to see Swiss charred. The man hadn't counted on the multilingual capacities of the natives, for by the time I arrived in the Bernese Oberland, two days later, all traces of his corpse had been eradicated. We suspect that he lies at the foot of the Reichenbach Fall. Only a study of his signature in the register at the local inn convinced me that he could not have been Paulding. Can you hear me down there?"

I was lying under his desk, with my head partially concealed in his overturned wastebasket, and I waved one hand feebly to indicate continuing consciousness.

"Similarly," Turtletaub continued, "the tragic affair of the Black Retainer *could* have been Quist-Squegg's work—or so I believed when I first investigated. The difficulty of playing a Negro butler with sufficient servile aplomb as to take in the entire Culpepper family, as well as the other plantation hands, is a challenge that would attract a great actor. Surely you remember the case—it led to the overnight revival of sixteen Klan chapters in South Carolina alone. My investigations on the scene, however, proved the unlikelihood of premeditation, and I had to absolve our two loonies of any involvement. To be sure, the aged retainer knew that his master, Colonel Gaylord Culpepper, was a hopeless alcoholic who regularly did away with fourteen mint juleps before lunchtime, but how could he have anticipated that on that particular day the Colonel, in stumbling search of another bottle of bourbon, would pass out in the pantry, crashing headlong in a welter of comestibles? And how could he have arranged matters so that, in his fall, the Colonel would pull down upon himself a two-pound, economy-size box of Hershey's Instant Cocoa? No, it was pure accident, and the missing butler—who has so far escaped apprehension—was but a chance victim suddenly struck down by this sinister new affliction. His mistress, you see, noting the absence of the family rumhound from the environs of the decanter, rang the bell, and when the courtly servitor had shuffled into the room she said, 'Cudjo, wheah's the Colonel?' How the poor fellow must have trembled as he saw the pit suddenly yawn at his feet! He could not help himself. He bowed and murmured, 'Massa's in de cocoa grounds.' "

I sprang up from under Turtletaub's desk, conking my head on the typewriter table, and flew to the window. "Air!" I gasped, clawing at the latch. "Give me air!"

"Yes, the airplane," Turtletaub continued, closing his eyes and forming a steeple with his fingers. "It's time to sum up. For all my efforts, Paulding-Moran and his evil partner remained undetected right up to the moment last month when their paths, by mad prearrangement, converged. Picture the drama. Paulding, in the pilot's seat, makes certain secret adjustments to the controls to destroy all navigational signals and diminish power. He alerts the passengers to their plight, and the 'lost' plane plummets toward its rendezvous on the hilltop. As the jet slithers across the grass, 'Brother Larry' bursts from hiding, dashes forward, and *pretends* to be struck down by the wing tip. The plane stops, the pilot coolly makes his report to the strapped-down passengers and crew, and, a moment later, he and his accomplice make good their escape, leaving half a hundred helpless victims in a condition of mass psycholepsy. *Finis.*"

" '*Finis*'?" I croaked. "But—but, what *happened*?"

Turtletaub looked at me for an instant, puzzled. "Oh," he said at last, "didn't I tell you before? After the plane stopped moving,

Paulding turned on the plane's intercom and announced, 'Well, folks, out of the flying plan and into the friar.' But, my dear fellow—" and with a troubled face he sprang toward me as I toppled forward gratefully into oblivion.

My champagne glass is empty; the plane dips toward Paris. My tale is nearly done. No need to recount the long, painful weeks of my illness, the battle for the cloudy fortress of my mind. Suffice it to say that while cleverly feigning coma one morning I overheard the rascally Turtletaub—that devoted "friend"! that defender of public weal!—plotting with a band of white-garbed quacks for my permanent sequestration! "I blame myself," the villain told them again and again. "I should have seen it coming."

What he should have seen coming was my escape, that very evening. What he could *never* have seen coming was my present guise, the nature of my forthcoming career, and—*hee, hee, hee!*— my name. Shall I offer you a peep at my passport? Very well— there! You start back in surprise. It cannot be, you think! Ah, but it is. Pray let me introduced myself—"Lionel Turtletaub," at your disposal.

Lionel Turtletaub, who, by means of certain cleverly dispatched and intercepted cables, will shortly begin tenure as a detective on loan to the Sûreté. There, with full access to criminal files, I shall find my first accomplice. A Chinese, a Malay perhaps—it doesn't matter; he need only be Oriental. Then, within weeks, I select my victim. Already I can see her—a pert Parisian widow, habituated to a certain elegance, perhaps a young vicomtesse. *Pauvre chérie,* she is soon to be troubled by a series of minor robberies. First a ring, then a brooch, then the *lavallière* once presented to her by the late vicomte himself. The police are called; a master detective, an American Maigret, comes forward to offer his services. Turtletaub to the rescue! There is another robbery, though, and then another. Madame is disconsolate, but M. l'Inspecteur vows to crack the case. He spends hours at her flat, examining fingerprints. A friendliness, a genuine warmth, seems to deepen between them. He offers certain gallantries; blushing, she dismisses them.

Then, on a warm night, Madame hears a sound, sees a shadow. She sits up in bed and screams! Through the French window springs Turtletaub, *pistolet* in hand. The trap has been sprung. His flashlight darts here, there, then focusses on the closet. A scuffle, an oath, and then out from behind Madame's dresses comes the criminal, hands high in the air. Still keeping him covered, Turtletaub snaps on the bedroom lights. The robber is wearing silk slippers, a long queue, and an angry Mandarin scowl. M. l'Inspecteur smiles at his distraught client, who charmingly pulls the coverlet higher toward her chin. Bowing, Turtletaub murmurs, "At last, Madame, I have discovered the Chink in your armoire!"

The no-smoking light is on: Paris. Paulding, *cher maître!* Quist, *mon semblable!* Ye shall be revenged!

Achievement

The Bureau of Accomplishments and Awards has received an enormous volume of submissions for the three-month period ending July 1st. Mankind's long striving for new world's records seems to have altered or widened, and now reaches for something beyond leviathan bass or pancake Everests. The Bureau, gratified but overworked, concludes that the urge for unique personal distinction has become universal. Although its full report must await the processing of late claims, several notable records and near-misses may now be announced.

Owen Duggan, 57, while taking a shower at home in his apartment on West Eighty-Fourth Street, on the morning of April 27th, accidentally dropped his cake of soap. Mr. Duggan reported later that he heard the unsurprising *thunk!* made by a cake of wet soap striking porcelain but noted the absence of any accompanying bouncing or slithering noises and also failed to feel the soap nudging his feet or ankles in customary post-fumble fashion. He then wiped the water from his face, opened his eyes, and saw said piece of soap seemingly affixed to the tub bottom *in a vertical stance.* Duggan instantly turned off the shower, thus cutting off the desecnding flow of warm water that, unchecked, would have quickly loosened the object from its resting place. Then, taking care not to dislodge the new monument with his feet, he drew back the shower curtain (translucent plastic, with a mauve dolphin motif), stepped out of the tub, opened the bathroom door, and called to his wife, Helen Duggan, 44, who was making breakfast in the kitchen. He invited her to hurry in and see something she would not wish to miss. It took several calls to persuade Mrs. Duggan to make the short journey, and she then expressed misgivings about entering the steam-filled bathroom in the presence of her towel-clad spouse. Owen Duggan was insistent, however, and in time Mrs. Duggan warily observed the still adherent cake of soap in its unusual posture.

Her first emotion, she has stated, was one of irritation and extreme, almost aggravated, unsurprise. Her second was doubt; to put it plainly, she accused her husband of deception. However, Duggan's outraged cries at this juncture caused her to withdraw this unpleasant demurrer, and she was persuaded that the inspiration to counterfeit such an unlikely happenstance was not within her husband's normal range of behavior.

The investigation was now further enlarged by the arrival in the bathroom of Douglas F. Duggan, 15, the son of the shower-taker, who made loud inquiries as to the meaning of the impromptu conference. At the urging of his parents, the young Duggan directed his attention toward the tub and saw that it contained a cake of soap that appeared to have balanced itself with force on the tip of its long axis.

Owen Duggan now took the opportunity to explain to the witnesses that the unique nature of the recent event depended in great part upon the brand of soap he had chanced to employ (and lose his grip on) in his ablutions. It was a well-known soap called Dove, and Dove, Duggan said, is "pointy at the ends." (The Bureau's Research Division, in confirmation, describes the typical cake of Dove as being oblong-ovate, and also slightly falcate, or sickle-shaped, along one axial plane.) "My drop," said Owen Duggan, for the first time employing the personal possessive, "wouldn't have meant a thing if the soap had of been one of those old boxy, squared-off soaps like Dial or Camay. Anybody could hit with one of those, sooner or later, but mine has got to be a world record."

Duggan *fils* now abruptly clasped his head in apparent pain and uttered a series of low cries. "Oh, wow!" he said. "Oh, wow! Who is going to *believe* this? I mean, this whole weird family all stuffed into this fantastic bathroom and staring at one weird little piece of soap! Oh, this family is too freaky, man. Wow." He withdrew.

Mrs. Duggan sighed and then bent over the tub once more and scrutinized the exhibit. "*Tchk!*—funny," she said musingly, and returned to the kitchen.

Owen Duggan turned on the water and resumed his shower.

A minute or two later, he experienced a distinct feeling of loss when he saw the cake of Dove topple over. He remained in the shower for eleven minutes more, repeatedly dropping the soap (which became softer, smaller, and quite battered in appearance) from shoulder-height and learning that even with careful aiming it is almost impossible to make a cake of Dove land on its tip, let alone stick there. When Duggan at last emerged from the bathroom, late for breakfast, his fingertips were wrinkled, but he was content.

Finding: A First in free soap-drop is confirmed, subject to counterclaims in this new record area.

Furman Krieger, 37, while playing tennis on Sunday, May 23rd, served a double fault at game point, 15–40, in the seventh game of the second set of the regular Sunday-afternoon men's doubles at Harry Lindermann's court in Wilton. It was Krieger's eighth double fault of the day, and it caused him and his partner, Amos Hedlund, to fall behind their opponents, Lindermann and Mel Fagen, by five games to two. Fagen and Lindermann had also won the first set, 6–3. Krieger has a fast sliced serve—*too* fast, in the opinion of some of his friends—which is very effective at times, but this year, what with the wet spring weather and all, he does not yet have it entirely under control. Carefully weighing these factors, Amos Hedlund remained in his position at net after his partner's second serve struck a good eight inches outside the service court, but took the precaution of slightly ducking his head and leaning almost imperceptibly toward the alley. Sure enough, in a moment there was a sharp report behind him, and Krieger's third service sailed past his head on its way into the syringa bushes on the far side of the Lindermanns' pool. Then there came an interesting whirring sound *(Whong-whungg! Whong-whungg!)* as Krieger's shiny new Wilson graphite racquet took wing like some enormous ornithopter, rotating rapidly and glittering in the sun as it ascended over the net, over the opposite court, and, prodigiously, over the high back fence, just ticking the top wire there ("Let!" cried Harry Lindermann) before it bounced in the driveway behind the court and disappeared under Mel Fagen's green Volvo wagon. The other players instantly agreed that this was not only Furman Krieger's finest racquet-fling in a long history of impulsive athletics but possibly a new Eastern double record for height and distance. Krieger, who was seen to be holding his right elbow in gingerly fashion, modestly accepted congratulations, but opined that he had probably made his final attempt at either record, since he had just thrown out his arm.

Finding: Claim postponed. The advent of steel and composition racquets has resulted in an avalanche of new statistics, many of which, if accepted, will make Krieger's throw appear distinctly commonplace. The Bureau has already announced that eventual new world and regional records achieved with these lighter, larger racquets will be listed with an accompanying asterisk, in order not to wipe out memories of famous marks set in the all-wood days. However, the Bureau did take note of the fact that Furman Krieger had already come to its attention three years ago, when he threw a sand wedge into the topmost branch of a willow tree eighty-two feet to the right of a fairway bunker on the fifth hole at Wee Spinney (the iron is still there, an object of local awe and superstition), and it has issued a Special Commendation to Mr. Krieger for two such memorable efforts in entirely separate fields of sporting endeavor.

Howard Lebo, 41, the lyricist, was eleven weeks late with the words for the title song for "Bad Creek," the new, sixties-revival, offbeat love-in-a-commune picture that had already gone four million over an extremely tight budget, with the result that everybody was very, very jumpy. Lebo, who is known in his business as a bleeder, hadn't been too worried, because shooting had fallen way behind (rain on location in Oregon), and besides, this wasn't a musical; all that was needed was a strong thematic lead-in—a four- or five-verse voice-over behind the titles. But now the word was in that they would wrap in another ten days, and the title people needed the finished theme right away, like *now*. It was Friday afternoon, and Lebo had been staring out of the window of his studio on West Fifty-third Street for an hour and twenty minutes. One of his troubles was that, although he had read the script, he still didn't know anything about communes. Another was that his composer, Jerry Monasch, had given him an unusually ambitious piece of music, very Burt Bacharach, with no release and four different tempo markings. Monasch was probably up at his summer place at Martha's Vineyard, and Lebo had his telephone number there, but he and Jerry hadn't been speaking for more than a month. Anyway, the real trouble was the title itself—a spondee: two bullets behind the ear. Lebo, watching a row of inert pigeons on the parapet of a litter-strewn roof across the street, felt more and more sorry for himself. Joseph Conrad should have had such troubles.

"I bet Irving Berlin never had to hack anything like this," Lebo said aloud. "Or Harold Rome, either."

The two names swam in the fetid air of the studio, and suddenly Lebo straightened up. "Hey," he said.

He went to his desk, threw the script and stack of scribbled notes on the floor, and began to write. Twenty minutes later, he picked up the telephone and called his agent, Otto Ness.

"Me, Otto," Lebo said. "You won't believe this. Listen." He read aloud to Ness from a piece of paper covered with names.

"What?" said Ness when Lebo had finished. "What, this is the *lyric*?"

"Wake up, Otto," said Lebo. "Don't you dig it? I'll read it again."

"Don't read it," said Ness hastily. "Now, listen to me, Howard. They've been on the phone all day from the Coast. My God, I told them you were polishing. They said Monday for sure, or—"

"Otto, all you understand is businessmen," Lebo said in a hurt tone. "This is the first creative thing I've done in months. Sure, it's only a beginning, but who knows? I'm thinking in Larry Hart terms—a little patter song for a charming O.B. revue."

"Howard!" Ness shouted.

"I'm going out to the island now," Lebo said placatingly. "You know I always work better out there. I'll have fifty verses for them tomorrow afternoon. There's nothing to worry about, Otto, I'm unblocked now."

"I'll call you tomorrow," Ness said.

"Make it Sunday."

•

At one o'clock the next afternoon, Saturday, Lebo, wearing a Mets cap and faded denim jeans, was sitting on a chaise longue on the sundeck of his beach cottage at Seaview. He had not started on the lyric for "Bad Creek," but the weekend was still young. What was needed now was a mood of high, easy confidence. A little laughter to cheer the lonely poet on his way. The Emmerichs, two cottages down, were coming over for drinks and a pickup lunch, and Lebo's wife, Kay, was neatening up on the sundeck. She was barefoot, in tan shorts and a ribbed white top. Lebo had been saving his list, but now he suddenly realized that Martin Emmerich would take it as another game, a challenge, and begin breaking in on him. Better not wait.

"Did I tell you I'm giving up writing?" he said to Kay. "I've decided to form a musical group."

"Classical or rock?" said Kay, knocking sand out of two canvas cushions.

"Hard to say," Lebo said. "I've already signed up John Denver and Whitney Houston as leads. I think I'll let her front it. We'll call it Whitney and the Metropoles."

"It doesn't sound like her sort of thing."

"I've inked three veteran sidemen already. Wilbur and Sidney de Paris and Ike Quebec."

"I don't think I know Ike Quebec," Kay murmured. She had been folding up the *Times* and she paused to read something.

"Tenor sax," Lebo said. "Guess who's going to write the theme for the group. Two people. Go ahead, guess."

"Why, I have no idea," Kay said, looking at him now.

"Irving Berlin and Harold Rome."

"But they're both—Oh, I see now. I should've known."

"Do you think Irving was East or West Berlin?" Lebo went on.

"I think West, don't you? Because that way, Isaiah Berlin can be East, see?"

"But Isaiah Berlin was never a musician," Kay said. "How does he—"

"Who said I was only forming an orchestra?" Lebo said, closing his eyes behind his shades. "I might just get up a squad of athletes, too. The Rand-McNally Globetrotters. Take 'em on tour. Joe Montana could be captain. Ralph Boston would have to be on it—the old broad jumper. And Claudell Washington. Leon Durham, used to play for the Cardinals. Benito Santiago. Pat Sheridan. Clyde Milan and Ted Lyons. All ballplayers. Marty Emmerich will *kill* himself over Ted Lyons. Ted *Lee*-yon."

Lebo became aware that his wife had left the sundeck. He got up and went to the bar table, under the shade of a yellow canvas awning, and rather irritably mixed himself a gin-and-tonic.

"I just sold my ballteam!" he called into the house. "I'm starting a film company instead. Douglas Fairbanks. Burt Lancaster. Sylvia Sidney."

"I know what your athletes eat at training table," Kay said, reappearing with plates and paper napkins.

"I'm talking about movies now," Lebo said. "Screenplay by Stephen Birmingham and William Manchester, from an idea by Racine."

"Brussels sprouts and Lima beans."

"That's *not* how this game is played," Lebo said, his voice rising. "Where was I? Oh, yes, Sylvia Sidney. She goes steady with Arthur Brisbane, the late journalist, who takes us, perhaps via Warren Moscow, into a politico-journalistic club whose members include Harold Washington, William Scranton, Harlan Cleveland, Harrison Salisbury, and, uh—*Grover* Cleveland, the late, much loved two-term Prez."

"You've forgotten Portland Mason and Portland Hoffa," said Kay, now making her own drink.

"God damn it to hell!" Lebo shouted. "I *knew* you'd get it wrong. How can you think even for an instant that I haven't ruled out all those easy first names? Cleveland Amory and Tennessee Williams—*any* idiot can do those. Dallas Townsend, Denver Lindley, Dallas Smith, Vermont Royster, Illinois Jacquet. You let them in, and the next thing you know you're ass-deep in people like Rochester and Buffalo Bill. The trouble with you, Kay, is you never set any standards for yourself."

Kay took her drink indoors.

"I don't see why you resent me for being good at this," Lebo said, leaning on the railing and staring off to sea. "The only reason I am is because it's sort of part of my work. Words. Wordsmithing. And besides, I wrote all these down yesterday, while I was working on the lyric."

"Did you finish it yet?" Kay said, coming back onto the sundeck with the salad bowl. "The picture thing?"

"Just one more name," Lebo said quickly. "He's my backer for the film company. Huntington Hartford. Great, hunh? I've thought about it, and there are no other names that can be added. I've come up with something special. I mean, I don't think anybody else has ever done this, do you?"

Kay placed a dish of cherry tomatoes on the porch railing next to her husband. She put her hands on his shoulders and bent close to him, as if she were about to kiss him on the ear. He smiled.

"Olga San Juan," she whispered.

Lebo seized a handful of cherry tomatoes, perhaps eight or ten in all, and drew back his arm. But then he only tossed two of them up in the air and ducked in under them, with his mouth open and his hands behind his back. It was his famous trick catch. The tomatoes were still up there, two dots of scarlet in the bright air, when the phone began to ring.

Finding: Honorable Mention in creative work-delay.

On the afternoon of June 9th, Frederick Tansill, 79, went to the movies in a theatre on upper Broadway. When his wife was alive, they hardly ever went to the movies, but now Tansill forced himself to go every week or two; it was a way of keeping up. Almost alone in the orchestra, he watched a French film. It was a rerun, a revived classic. There was a young woman in long skirts; there was a tall dark man and a shorter blond man. They wore narrow, old-fashioned clothes. The time in the film was long ago. There were many short scenes—the woman (called Catherine) and the two men drinking together, the woman dressing up like a boy and the tall man painting a mustache on her face, the woman and the two men at separate windows of a white house in the country. Tansill tried to follow the story without reading the English subtitles, but he could not understand more than a few phrases of the dialogue. He had lived in Paris on three separate occasions, once for a stretch of almost two years, and now suddenly he could no longer understand spoken French. Another piece knocked off him. A scene on bicycles: Catherine wore a white blouse and a white scarf tied up over her hair, the blond man wore a small cap; they were at the beach. Immediately afterward, at night, Catherine jumped off an embankment into the Seine, and the two men helped her out of the water. Now Tansill began reading the subtitles, but he had missed too much of the story. On the screen, the First World War began.

Tansill must have dozed, for now Catherine seemed to have a young daughter. (Asleep, all by himself, in this frightful theatre?) There was a hill covered with long grasses, and the little girl and the taller man rolled down the hillside in each other's arms. Tansill was trying to remember the name of a young woman in a white blouse and long white skirt. It had been years and years ago, but he could see her face perfectly. Suddenly it was like a window going up. He was sitting on a porch with her in the country, in Tamworth, and they were waiting for the rain to stop. His bicycle was leaning against a porch pillar, under the eaves. He had been caught in the rain, on his way somewhere on the bike. The porch pillars were square and covered with gray shingles, like the rest of the house. He must have been fourteen or fifteen years old.

On the screen, Catherine was playing a guitar and singing to the others. The young woman in the long white skirt looked a little like her, but she had had darker hair. It was the Harders' house, of course, just at the top of the steep dirt lane. The rain had caught him and he had run for it. The young woman—she was a girl, really—must have heard him running up the porch steps and laughing. She had come out of the house, carrying a mandolin in one hand, and the screen door bumped shut behind her. "Oh, you must be Freddie Tansill," she said. "Look, you're *soaked*." He knew her. She was a cousin of Laurie Harder's and a friend of his own sister, Marian. Maybe four years older than he was. What was her name? Catherine's song was over. Now she was kissing the tall man. Or was it another man?

The Harders were all away somewhere for the day. No one else in the house. The two of them sat in green rocking chairs and watched the rain spilling down from the overflowing gutters along the eaves of the deep porch. The thunder had gone grumbling up the valley, and already you could see the sky lightening above the birches and the clouds moving off the face of Passaconaway. The girl was holding the mandolin on her lap; two green velvet ribbons hung down from its neck. "Can you play that thing?" he asked. "Marian has one, but all she can do is plunk on it."

To his surprise, she began at once to play the mandolin. In a low, gentle voice, she sang a song in some foreign language. He didn't recognize any of the words, but the song must have been Italian, for he had just remembered being told that Laurie Harder's cousin had spent a whole year in school in Italy. He had never heard anyone play and sing to him, alone like this, and he was afraid to look at her. Her left foot, resting on the grass matting of the porch, was crooked up, the heel raised to support her crossed right leg and the mandolin. She wore pale-tan sneakers. The green velvet ribbons moved slightly on her white skirt as she picked out the quick music. What was her name? She stopped, laughing a little, and when Tansill only nodded two or three times she said, "Well, maybe you know this one," and began to play again. He did know it, but he could not make himself sing with her when she got to the chorus:

"Waltzes, polkas, lancers, galops, glides,
Portland fancy, quadrilles and reels and slides,

High-lows, didoes—How we danced 'em all!
I'll never forget the time, you can bet,
We went down to Odd Fellows Hall!"

This time when she finished, he asked her where she had got such a fancy mandolin. Time was passing. On the screen, Catherine had grown older; she was wearing small, round eyeglasses and a white cloche hat.

"In Genoa," she said. "Look, you can see the name here inside."

She turned the mandolin around, tipping it toward the afternoon light, and together they peered into the round sound hole under the strings. There was a label down inside, with gold lettering, and as he tried to read it he felt her dark hair brush against his arm. Her name was Evangeline. Evangeline Courtald.

Tansill said the name out loud, and a young couple two rows ahead of him turned right around to look at him. "Oh, get along with you," he said sharply. And then, but now speaking only to himself, he added, "I am the last person in the history of the world who will ever think of Evangeline Courtald's mandolin."

Finding: No cause for an award is discerned. In the Bureau's judgment, memory is ever unique and thus undistinguishing. Solipsism is not encouraged. Regrets.

The Exegesis of St. Nick

(Another Frightful Bloodletting in the Back Alleys
of the *New York Review of Books*)

To the Editors:

Nothing could be more flattering to a scholar than to have a
work of his reviewed by so eminent an expert as Hermann Kronstadt, but candor forces me to confess a total lack of surprise
when I discovered that Professor Kronstadt had in fact barely
bothered to read my little exegesis of "A Visit from St. Nicholas"
(*Clement Moore and the Pre-Keynesian Apocalypse*, Pottawattamie
A. & M. University Press, $15) but had chosen instead merely
to add some footnotes to his own tediously celebrated post-
Freudian studies of the sexually feudalistic substratum in American children's books—a lode that so clearly ran out in the early
chapters of his recent *Wynken, Blynken and Nod's Narrenschiff: Anal
Archetypes on a Sea of Guilt*. If this were all, I would remain silent,
for students of Victorian Americana have long since discovered
that Professor Kronstadt thinks he has the horse-and-buggy
Christmas safely locked away in his own curious clinic; he is the
Molochian lump of coal that lies at the bottom of every young
scholar's stocking. But Herr Kronstadt has gone too far in his
ill-tempered review in your colomns, for he has not only ob-
durately refused to accept the *Ding an sich* of my modest pos-
tulates but has launched on a course of reckless misinterpretation
and misquotation that I can only regard as intentional. To para-
phrase his testy penultimate aphorism ("If Bertrand Russell was
not Hölderlin, Dr. Swiggett is certainly not Karl Mannheim"), I
would murmur that though I am not Mannheim, Professor

Kronstadt may be more of a Nietzsche than even he or Max Weber would care to admit!

To be specific. I did not not suggest, or even *fail* to suggest, that the "Mama in her kerchief and I in my cap" *mise an scène* contained a "swaddled, nunlike repression of Clement Moore's unacceptably ravening id." I would not agree with this irresponsible bit of wildfire hermeneutics even if I had thought of it myself. Careful readers of my book will remember that my only comments on these early lines of the poem were those expatiating upon the profound sadness of doomed *laissez-faire* capitalism as sounded in the "visions of sugarplums danced through their heads" (*die Entzauberung der Zuckerpflaume,* in my phrase) image; plus, a bit later, my chapter dealing with the unbidden but frighteningly intrusive noises emanating from the overworked New England textile factories, and the concomitant din of rising industrial Jacobinism, that break in upon the narrator's long Victorian sleep: "When out on the lawn there arose such a clatter . . ."

I think it is typical of Professor Kronstadt's well-known vendetta style of criticism that he should concentrate in his review upon my careless but entirely insignificant omission of Prancer from the list of the reindeer (why did I not omit the equally androgynous Cupid or Dancer, Herr Kronstadt?), while he neglects all mention of my fruitful *propositio,* first suggested to me by Dietrich Maltby at the Determinism Workshop of 1965, that "Dasher, Dancer, Prancer & Vixen/Comet, Cupid, Donder & Blitzen" are, in fact, evidence of Clement Moore's desperate need for economic reassurance and moral book-balancing in a time of stress, through the agency of the sudden arrival of two thinly disguised Wall Street law firms on his rooftop.

I have further reservations, equally documented, about Professor Kronstadt's anti-critical fugue, but I will suppress them, if only in deference to the happy season. These would include an anguished protest against his charge that I have "failed utterly to deal with Moore's infantilistic anti-Semitism as seen in the transliteration and apotheosis of 'that good Protestant clubman called St. Nicholas' out of the blatantly obvious paradigm of the

Wandering Jew known as Claus"; I deal with precisely that problem in my footnote on the "he looked like a pedlar just opening his pack" simile, and later, at further length, in my discussion of the inflationary rise of St. Nick up the chimney after the dividend distribution on the hearth, and the mysterious but unmistakably Faginesque gesture "laying his finger aside of his nose." (J. S. W. Turgeon and P. Rabbitt both suggest that this digital kinesis descends from the Hasidic finger-ritual *yodh-zahim,* but I am dubious.) Professor Kronstadt evidently failed to read that far in my book. That failure, so typical of those who continue to refuse to come to terms with the giant problem of the undistributed middle, disqualifies him as a Leavisite, or even as a backwoods Hobbesian, and certainly as a critic worthy of your pages.

Geoffrey Palamore Swiggett

Pottawattamie A. & M. University
Cornflake, Iowa

Hermann Kronstadt *replies:*

I wish to apologize to Dr. Swiggett for my inadvertent attribution of the "swaddled, nunlike" repression of the oh-so-good sleeping burghers of poor Clement Moore's jingle to him. That fragment of deft scholarship was, in fact, contained in an assigned "My Holidays" theme by one of my freshman students here at Redwood Poly; the paper was lying on my desk at the time that I wrote my review, so the mistake, though risible, is perhaps understandable. Actually, it's a pity that such an insight was not in Dr. Swiggett's book, for it struck me as by far the keenest *aperçu* I had read of the work in question, and might have led our unhappy author to a more fructuous harvest of conclusions.

Dr. Swiggett's semi-hysterical objections to my review suggest the anxieties of a cloistered exegete when he happens on an unexpected work of pseudepigrapha. He seems to blame me, rather than himself, for his book, and I would remind him quietly that the ideological equivalent of double agency, however unwitting, is antiquated Hegelian dialectic. After reading his letter, I must conclude that what seemed to be a mere failure to see (Kant's *Nichtverstehen*), is, in fact, a terrified refusal to know. Dr. Swiggett is an economist, but even economists have an unconscious, as Eriksen and George Lichtheim have agreed. His pathetic insistence on the little string of leftover Lekachmanisms that so entangles his work does not constitute a reply to the perfectly cheerful suggestions I made about Clement Moore's dark night of the soul; those dancing sugarplums *are* prepubertal phantasies, for all that Dr. Swiggett, with the blankets pulled up to his nose, insists that they are Bryanesque bags of free silver!

Why doesn't Dr. Swiggett attempt to answer my questions? What is he afraid of? His jiggery-pokery about New England textile mills does not hide the fact that "When out on the lawn there arose such a clatter" can *only* have been inspired by the then newly invented lawnmower, and thus constitutes another unconscious recrudescence of the sexual machine, the phallic juggernaut, that so troubled the dreams of our grandparents. At the risk of repeating myself, I would point out to Dr. Swiggett that only a dangerously overburdened superego could keep him from accepting that "Away to the window I flew like a flash,/ Tore open the shutters and threw up the sash./The moon on the breast of the new-fallen snow/Gave the luster of midday to objects below" all too vividly describes an imperfectly sublimated vision of marital divestiture and defloration—perhaps of a less healthy nature than that which Melanie Klein discovered in "The Eve of St. Agnes." Can his conveniently forgotten Prancer and his strangely flying law firms obfuscate the preorgasmic urgency of "Now Dasher, now Dancer, now Prancer and Vixen,/On Comet, on Cupid, on Donder and Blitzen!"? Come, come, Dr. Swiggett, this is the twentieth century! Please join us in the ranks of the *libérés*, who remember that, in Ferenczi's words, "Only confirmed Oedipals insist that the penalty for *la trahison des clercs* is life imprisonment." Or are you afraid to ascend "to the top of the porch, to the top of the wall" and then "dash away, dash away, dash away all!"?

In the spirit of the season, I will close by pointing out that I have certainly not refused to accept the *donnée* of Dr. Swiggett's clumsily wrapped but charming little hand-woven potholder. I wish only to suggest, to him and to your readers, that Great Granddaddy Clement Moore's familiar old mahogany whatnot casts some startling shadows when held up to the strong light of intelligence!

The Great Starch Debate

(The Author of *Six Crises* Begins the Long Climb
Upward from 1962)

My experience has taught me that the first step in facing a crisis
is the ability to recognize that the crisis does in fact exist. This
requires a cool head and considerable personal background in
crisis-recognition. Looking back on it now, I am certain that no
one in our group but I sensed that a full-scale crisis was in the
making on that warm evening, early in my campaign for the
governorship of my native state, when we returned to our hotel
and I discovered that my shirts had not come back from the
laundry. We had enjoyed a busy and deeply satisfying day of
campaigning in the upper San Fernando Valley. I had made a
number of hard-hitting points in thirteen separate speeches, and
from the emotional point of view I had had the always enriching
experience of shaking hands with hundreds of folks who seemed
decidedly pleased with the principles I had made perfectly clear
to them. It had been another mountaintop experience, and after
it was over, there was a distinct temptation for my campaign
staff and me to relax momentarily and indulge ourselves in the
luxury of retrospection and self-congratulation. My discovery,
at this juncture, that my shirts had not come up from the laundry
was at first only an irritation. I had exhausted my small personal
stock of clean white shirts in the previous few days on the road,
and the hotel laundry had made a firm commitment to me of
delivery by 5 P.M. I had made it entirely clear to them that I
required a clean shirt for that evening, when I was scheduled
to address a Republican Peach-Pickers' Rally and then to par-

ticipate in a brass-tacks public debate on the issue of water fluoridation in parochial schools. When a thorough search of my suite turned up no package of clean shirts, I knew I had to take decisive action. I got busy on the telephone, speaking in person first to the front desk, then to the laundry room. Were my shirts ready? If not, would they be ready within the next hour?

Answer: negative. No one appeared to know where my shirts were. I hung up.

My estimate of the situation sharpened. As I sat by the bedroom telephone, engaged in inner debate, Earl Mazo, Bill Key, Alvin Moscow, Don Hughes, Jim Bassett, and several other members of my team came in. They sensed that something was "up." I quickly spelled out the facts for them and asked them for their evaluations. I told them I wanted advice, not sugar-coating.

The gist of their group opinion was at first glance both sensible and attractive. They urged me to take the easy way, to ride with the punch. They pointed out that a search for the shirts and a full disclosure of the reasons for their disappearance could be time-consuming and, in the long run, frustrating. They outlined the potential political dynamite that could be touched off if some member of our press entourage got wind of any "scene" that might ensue if I determined to follow through personally and find my shirts in the hotel. Several opinions pinpointed the fact that I could still in all probability go out and buy a new shirt before the beginning of the evening schedule. At least two of my companions kindly offered to lend me one of their own clean shirts—a warm expression of personal loyalty that I still cherish. As far as content went, their advice was excellent.

Nevertheless, I asked them to leave me alone for a few minutes while I made a deeper evaluation. I explained to them that a leader must do more than count the noses of his advisers. Left alone, I realized that I would be fully pardoned if I came to the conclusion that the situation I faced lay in one of life's gray areas, where the easier decision was called for. But there were principles involved, and I knew that any man who shirked the inner struggle at a time like this was guilty of irresponsibility. I saw at once that this was a crisis of an entirely new kind. This was not simply a case of Nixon being inconvenienced by the carelessness of one hotel or one laundry. If I were to permit myself to be bluffed out at this stage, it would mean that a citizen was acquiescing to the inefficiencies that woolly-thinking apologists often declare to be an innate part of the American system. It would be a case of Nixon putting his tail between his legs and surrendering to bureaucracy. I could not in conscience take such a course and then go before the people as their candidate. My philosophy has always been to do what is right. My instinct in this case was to act, to find the shirts.

Once I saw the course I had to take, any tension I might have felt disappeared. Courage—that is, the absence of fear—comes from conviction. I had long since learned that the decision-making process—that is, thinking—is the most trying part of any crisis. Now that my mind was made up, I felt cool and ready for battle. But merely to be doubly sure, I put long-distance calls through to Herb Brownell, Tom Dewey, Allen Dulles, and Charlie Halleck. All of them concurred, in broad terms, with the wisdom of my decision, and Charlie added that I had again made him proud to be an American. Tom Dewey was most specific. "This is a matter you must decide for yourself, Dick," he stated.

I summoned my staff back into the room. Quickly I laid the program before them. We would act, I said, because we were on the right side. But we would act responsibly, after thorough preparation and with proper human respect for the workings of the hotel's administrative apparatus. I asked them to prepare the necessary background material I would require, including data on laundry operations in general in the Free World, average delivery time of shirts by non-private launderers, wages and working conditions enjoyed by union and non-union ironers and folders, and so forth. I asked them to have this material before me in fifteen minutes, which would allow me perhaps another fifteen minutes for a crash briefing and intensive homework before we swung into action. They hurried off eagerly, and then for the first time I allowed myself to relax for a moment and reflect on what curious but perennially stimulating encounters history continued to place before the man who had once, back in a plain boy's bedroom in Yorba Linda, allowed his modest daydreams to encompass only the possibility of one day making the high-school junior-varsity debating team. Now, as far as background was concerned, the stage was set for that encounter that the American press, with more enthusiasm than accuracy, was later to call the Great Starch Debate.

Accompanied by two of my aides, I stepped into the elevator, turned, and faced the front of the car. "Laundry room, please," I said in a firm voice. The operator stole a puzzled glance at me, but I looked straight ahead. As we went down, I took stock of my physical condition. I was a trifle edgy, my palms were damp, and there was an empty feeling in the pit of my stomach. I suppose some might say that I was "nervous," but by drawing on personal experience I was able to recognize and even welcome these signs for what they were—the symptoms of a normal man in descent in a fast elevator.

We alighted in the sub-basement and I strode directly through the doors of the laundry room. I was at once enveloped in clouds of steam, but my painstaking briefing had prepared me for this eventuality, and I did not hesitate. In spite of the steam and the hiss and roar of washers and pressing machines, I was able to single out my man, the laundry manager, at once. He was behind a counter, wearing a white undershirt and white trousers. I introduced myself, and we shook hands. While our aides grouped themselves around us in the manner prescribed by protocol and roughed out between them the substance of the conversations to come, I took stock of my man. He exuded an unmistakable impression of weariness and ennui. Here, I knew, was a powerful adversary—a hard-core laundry manager, steeled to complaints, magnificently trained in evasion.

I got off to a particularly good start by pointing out to him that his failure to deliver my shirts constituted a breach of contract. In effect, I told him, he had failed to live up to his end of one of those countless small but vital agreements that permit men of good will to function together in our increasingly complex world.

He feigned bewilderment. The delivery of shirts was not in his province, he stated—only their processing.

Instinctively, I knew I had to press my attack. I asked him if he ever had any difficulty sleeping at night if he knew that even one of his customers felt less than complete satisfaction with the laundry service that day. I roughed out for him a broad panoramic view of the operations of our vast mercantile system and its concomitant and essential service subdivision.

He seemed reluctant to debate the points I had raised. He pounded the counter and, with some vivid and distinctly non-diplomatic peasant adages, stated that I was adding to, rather than clarifying, our differences.

My intensive preparations allowed me to absorb and counter his attack without being thrown off balance. I knew that from the standpoint of temper control this would be the worst possible time for me to blow my stack. I decided to shift tactics. An "end run" was called for. I pointed out that while over fifty-one million American males owned white shirts the average per-capita ownership (including steelworkers) was still only 2.3 shirts each, a figure that did not allow for any slipups in the laundry-processing industry. *Time* magazine later characterized this as "a beefed-up riposte that scored heavily in the drama."

Now it was his turn to change the pace. Forcing a laugh, he asked me if I was not being guilty of obscurantism.

"That's not my way," I retorted. "I shall never be guilty of obscurantism."

He poked a pudgy finger at me. "We are capable of dialectics, too, you know," he said menacingly.

Now we were going at it hammer and tongs. I was vaguely aware that a considerable crowd of laundresses, waiters, bellboys, and house detectives had surrounded us. None of them had ever heard anything like this before behind the doors of their laundry room, and I knew that even if I failed now in my primary mission, my journey would not prove to have been entirely in vain.

At this moment, one of the manager's assistants pressed a note into his hand. We both paused, panting in the steam, while he read its contents. He hesitated. "It seems," he said at last, "that your laundry has been found. It is in this room. Our position has been entirely justified. Your shirts are washed and ironed, but they have been detained here for reprocessing, because in inadvertence the starch was omitted. You will have them to-morrow, starched."

The day was won. Without knowing it, he had played directly into my hands, but years of experience in dealing with success now warned me that this was the time for magnanimity, not crowing. Smiling, I quoted to him Abraham Lincoln's remark, made in reference to one of his generals, that he preferred "starch in the man rather than in his shirt." It was my way of telling him that I never have my own shirts ironed with starch.

The manager shrugged. He turned, received the package of shirts from an assistant, and handed them to me. We shook hands warmly. Although the one-hundred-per-cent-successful outcome of our meeting had been largely unexpected, I was not unprepared even for this eventuality. Still holding his hand, I clapped him on the shoulder and said, "Isn't it fine that two men, each trained to a peak of creative usefulness by our great system of economic and personal incentives, can meet as we have and exchange views openly and without fear, thus adding to man's centuries-long struggle for understanding and freedom?"

He nodded wordlessly, and we parted. I turned and walked toward my elevator, ignoring the confused babble of voices be-hind me engaged in excited interrogation, recapitulation, and speculation. I pressed the elevator button. As I stood there, it occurred to me that many American men in their middle years might be suddenly depressed to find themselves, immediately after a personal success, standing in a hotel sub-basement with a package of laundry in their arms. I knew, however, that the most dangerous part of any crisis is its aftermath, the time of letdown. This is when the human system, wearied by tension and hyperbole, is all too apt to become exhausted and to indulge itself in destructive reflection. This knowledge enabled me to put the thought aside. I watched the needle on the indicator above the elevator door. The car was moving downward, but soon, I knew, it would rise again, taking me with it.

AFTERWORD TO *"The Great Starch Debate"*

That elevator that Mr. Nixon was waiting for at the end of this chapter did pick him up and, after a bumpy start, carried him all the way to the top floor—an ascent beyond the dreams of parody, and still, in retrospect, one that only the author of Six Crises *could have found entirely unhilarious. Absolute humorlessness has always been a formidable political asset in this country, and Mr. Nixon continues to prove almost to this day that his was the absolute gift. It was a shame in a way to watch him waste his stuff on the Presidency, for the wholly literal mind is so rare a comedy resource that it should be fenced off, labelled, visited, photographed at dawn and sunset, and honored in the guidebooks, like the Grand Canyon. What we have here, in short, is another failure of conservation. In time, of course, the great flood of Watergate overwhelmed and washed away Mr. Nixon's noble ponderosity, but from this distance we can look back at those stone escarpments and immense deadpan flats and try to remind ourselves what we lost.*

Sad Arthur

(Go Hesse, Young Man)

One morning, Sad Arthur, the banker's son, rose and garbed himself. Softly and lovingly the bedroom Mazdas bathed him as, supple-limbed, he drew on the new costume of his decision. Over his baggy BVD gaiters Sad Arthur put on his resplendent Belstaff Riding Suit with its storm-proof pockets, storm-cuff sleeves, heavy-duty zipper, snapdown pockets, and buckled mandarin-style collar. Sad Arthur bent and stepped into his Beau Geste Rough Rider boots with full-zippered backs, adjustable heel and instep straps, and imbedded front-and-back steel friction plates. Sad Arthur pulled on his Leathertogs genuine-leather jacket with transverse zipper and heavy-duty wrist snaps, and strapped on his stud wristbands and seven-inch stud belt. Delicately Sad Arthur balanced his yellow Foster Grants above his lofty brow and then picked up his flocked fuchsia Fury Helmet. Sad Arthur's mirror, which loved him unquenchably, watched in sad surprise as Sad Arthur left the bedroom forever. Then the mirror fell into a reflective mood, wondering once again how it had ever lost Altman's.

Sad Arthur entered the veranda and stood behind the chair where his father, the banker, was catching a few z's. The good banker, who that week had taken a bath in Leasco, was having a troubled dream about unholy ablutions. In time, he awoke, aware of the presence of leather. "Is that you, Sad Arthur?" he said.

Sad Arthur remained silent, his arms folded. Long ago, he had learned the lesson of the closed yap, the magic of the monosyllable. In the sullen, downward-hanging head, the lidded eye, the unheeding ear, there lay invulnerable peace. There was strange power in this youthful demeanor that willed nothing. Faced with it, the others—the teachers and talkers—became irritated, then flustered, then enraged, then placating, then suppliant. Like a flock of bees, they gave up their golden treasure to him who merely seemed to doze by the hive. So Sad Arthur stood unmoving. Sunbeams meditated in the unshorn locks on his neck.

"What is it already?" the banker demanded. "Come around here where I can see you." He sighed. "No—on second thought, don't."

"You know what is in my mind," Sad Arthur said at last. "I would leave home and join the Holy Terrors. Like."

"I don't get it," confessed the good banker. "My son the bike freak."

"With the Holy Terrors I will make Vegas," Sad Arthur said. "I wish to attain Nevada."

The banker fell silent. In his secret heart he, too, had seen himself joyful at Vegas, strolling The Sands. Several hours passed in silence, like skipped pages in a meaty volume. In time, the banker gave a start, opened his eyes, yawned, and rose from his chair. "Let me know if you attain Nevada," he said to his son. "Call us collect." He could deny nothing to this young man. Like the Mazdas and the mirror and the sunbeams, like everything and everybody, he loved Sad Arthur, though often it was hard to know why.

Sad Arthur left his home. Near the garage, his faithful companion Irving was waiting with the bikes.

"You have come," Irving said.

"I have come," said Sad Arthur, smiling.

"He was faked out," Irving said.

"He was faked out," said Sad Arthur.

"We can split," Irving said.

"We can split," said Sad Arthur.

They split.

•

Wandering westward, Sad Arthur and Irving found the Holy Terrors in a blighted grove near Leonia, N.J. They recognized the leader of the band, the fabled Guttheimer, and drew near. This good buddy was known for his teachings and his freaky vines. His ancient bombardier's jacket was encrusted with many a graffitic virtu and many a mottoed malediction, now all faded by wind and dust, that depicted the pain and suffering of the pilgrim's way. The Illustrated One, at ease astride his ancient Harley two-stroke banger, listened to Sad Arthur's and Irving's joyful plea to get their heads together as novitiates in the Holy Terrors, heard their deep desire to attain Nevada. He subjected them to certain rites and then, well pleased, grunted the wished-for grant. Sad Arthur and Irving were Holy Terrors at last!

Happy among brothers, boot to boot with these heavy-footed disciples and their Old Ladies, Sad Arthur wandered westward (and sometimes eastward and ditchward) on the ancient paths of Jersey. Together, the Holy Terrors bombed Bogota, deafened Dumont, horrified Hoboken, outraged Oradell, paralyzed Palisades Park, piqued Parsippany, ravaged Rahway, and were busted in Boonton. Here, within a rustic slammer, Sad Arthur drew near Guttheimer and spoke what was in his mind.

Sad Arthur said: "Hear me, O Illustrated One, for I am, you know, like troubled. I have heard your teachings and learned much. You show the world unbroken, like a well-lubed chain. From you I have learned the Eightfold Path to hop a Honda 90cc SL to a sassy quarter in thirteen with a stroker kit, trochoid pump, overboring, and velocity stacks. From you I have learned the Fivefold Path to dirty up a square Moto Guzzi 750cc Ambassador by means of laid-on chromed riser bars, extended forks, sissy bar, and STP decals. From you I have learned the Fourteenfold Path to cowboy-roll a joint while drafting on a downhill Greyhound at eighty per. All this have I learned, O Good Buddy, yet what do I see? I see this band still mucking about here in upper Jersey, no nearer Vegas than the day I fell in. So what are teachings, what is knowledge, what are dead eardrums and dropped kidneys if they do not take me to Nevada? Are you not, then, the same as my father the good banker, a mere workahubby?"

The Illustrated One's eyes were lowered, his furred mouth set in an unfathomable half-smile of understanding. He was stoned. "You are some punkins, O Sad Arthur," he said. "You are a real smart-ass. I would enlighten you with still another lesson, the Onefold Path to a bust in the mouth, only right now I gotta crash."

The next morning, Sad Arthur took his leave of the pokey. He bade farewell to the Holy Terrors. He bade farewell to the faithful Irving, who was crying. Alone, he wandered westward on his Kawasaki Three. He saw many things. He saw a small boy at a Carvel stand who had dripped chocolate ripple all over his mother's handbag. He saw a man in madras Bermudas who had just been bilked by a used-lawnmower salesman. He saw a young opossum that had just been mashed by a teen-ager in a magenta Corvette. He saw a drunken housewife weeping in front of her Sylvania color console. He saw an elderly pastor playing miniature golf in a black hairpiece. He saw a Fruehauf twelve-wheel rig lying on its side, with its cargo of disposable diapers scattered across the highway. The world was beautiful when seen this way—alone and without questions or meaning. It was beautiful to go through the world like this in childlike cool. The Illustrated One was right, Sad Arthur thought. Sad Arthur, you are some punkins.

In a sun-dappled launderette in Nutley, N.J., but a short distance from the holy ruins of the Nutley Velodrome, Sad Arthur encountered the fair Lambie, whose lips were like unto a melting Tootsie Roll. At one sight of her, he plugged in his Fender and, without thought or further ado, sang this song:

> "For love of the fair Lambie,
> The pilgrim Sad Arthur,
> Sad Arthur the erstwhile Terror,

The fabled rubber-layer,
Would forget Nevada
And stay
Here in Nutley Enn Jayyy!"

"O Sad Arthur, how marvie!" cried the entranced Lambie.

"Yes," said Sad Arthur without unbecoming modesty. "Please note the rhyme."

"O Sad Arthur, c'mere." She drew him to her, placing one heel on his instep and one hand on his ear in the position of love that is known as "Opening the Deck Chair." Then she kissed him with her lips that were like unto a melting Tootsie Roll.

Thus it was that Sad Arthur put away his boots and helmet, put away Nevada, put away his dreams and his Kawasaki to stay in Nutley and groove with the fair Lambie. He cut his hair and went to work for Lambie's father, a merchant, the owner of the Nutley Kwik Kleen Dry Cleaners. He went among the people and took on the people's ways. With Lambie, he bought six-packs and electric back-yard rotisseries, he wore His-'n-Hers flowered at-home jams, he joined the Thursday Evening Swingin' Couples League at Nutley Bowlorama. Lambie's father was pleased with him and said, "You have learned much from me, Sad Arthur."

"No," said Sad Arthur. "All that I have learned I have taught myself. I have learned to deliver a suit on Friday that was promised for Wednesday. I have learned to deliver size forty-two pants to the size thirty-four next door. I have learned to mislay ladies' dress belts, to anneal zippers, and to loosen buttons so that they will pop off upon being buttoned. I have learned to starch alpaca sweaters and imprint indelible rust stains on dress evening shirts. Most of all, I have learned the imperious Brahmin's manner that elicits abject thanks and excessive tips. Thus do I add injury and interest to the lives of these sad schnooks. It is you, rather, who have learned from me."

Lambie's father looked on Sad Arthur with admiration and surprise. "The mouth, O Sad Arthur," he said. "That mouth will get bust wide open one of these days."

Sad Arthur saw that it was time for him to resume his questing. The merchant's message, so like the parting words of Guttheimer, told him that he had come full circle. He had learned the people's ways, their business and their pleasures, and now his soul was sickened, as the soul of one who has played thrice at tick-tack-toe. He went to the fair Lambie and imparted unto her what he had decided.

"O no, Sad Arthur!" cried the fair Lambie. She placed her elbow in his abdomen and her knee against his back, in the position that is known as "Putting Away the Ironing Board," but he pushed her rudely aside.

"Tough darts, Lambie," Sad Arthur said. "It's Nevada for me. Bye now."

Why did her lips, curved in sorrow, remind him of a Cat's Paw heel?

Sad Arthur turned westward once more. On foot now, he wandered with thumb lifted, riding with any who heeded his disdainful summons. Riding silent in high cab beside some trusting trucker, Sad Arthur smiled and commended himself for having put aside still more knowledge, more habits, more mere humans. Within his stomach he felt the tiny gerbil of his Self stirring once again, heard it remount its squeaky little wheel.

Closer to Vegas at last, Sad Arthur alighted on the north bank of the great Pennsylvania Pike, and here took employment as night pumper in a modest Amoco station. Wearing the plain blue coveralls and friendly smile of his humble calling, he dispensed the golden fluid, wiped clean the insect-speckled windshield, kept track of the ladies'-room key with its giant tag. At night, between customers, he tilted back in his chair and listened to the highway. He knew he should resume his journey, should seek Nevada, yet it seemed to him that this highway had something to tell him. He felt a deep love for these broad humming lanes with their upping and downing, their easting and westing, their freight of fumes and destinations, and he sat and stayed and listened.

Years passed, and so it was at last that an ochre Caddy stopped at Sad Arthur's modest Amoco station and yielded up a bald old gent with low back pains and a large cigar. Sad Arthur looked on him and smiled.

"Sad Arthur!" cried the old gent. "Is that you? Are you here, only here? And all this time I imagined you at Nevada!"

"Yes," said Sad Arthur. "It is I, my old friend. Only I."

"What a gas!" cried the faithful Irving (for it was he), and then he laughed at his own foolish wit. "So neither of us made it to Vegas, eh? What a pair of losers!"

"Listen, my friend," said Sad Arthur, and he took Irving by the arm and led him closer to the highway's edge. "Listen to me, for I have learned the secret. The highway was taught me all. At one end of this highway, back beyond its beginning, is my father, the good banker. There too are the Illustrated One, the fair Lambie, the overturned diaper truck, my rusted old Kawasaki, and the lost size forty-two pants. At the other, beyond its ending and yet part of it as well, lies Nevada. At the same time, right now, they are all part of this highway, all one. This highway is everywhere at the same moment—the toll-taker and the toll-payer, the patient concrete and the headlong tire, the descendant swallow-dropping and the approaching open convertible, the totalled Pontiac and the greedy wrecker, the full box of Goobers on the dashboard and the emptied box of Goobers in the weeds by the roadside. This highway is the beginning and the ending, the cool and the uncool, learning and forgetting, the book revered and the book flung halfway across the room. There is no truth, no knowing, no wisdom, no Nevada, no nothing except, uh—well, simultanuity, like. So relax."

"Gosh, Sad Arthur," said Irving. "I never thought of it that way." He looked at his watch. "Well, Artie," he said hastily, "this has been real. Any time you're near Hasbrouck Heights—"

But again Sad Arthur drew him closer to the highway's edge. "Listen, faithful Irving," Sad Arthur said. "Listen to the highway. What does it say to you?"

"Well," said Irving after a while, "it sort of says 'Zoom!' "

"Yes," said Sad Arthur. He lifted his head in wonder. "Zoom!" he repeated. "Zoom-*zoom!*"

L'Après-Midi d'un Fan

(Sundays, Up Close and Long Ago)

ANNOUNCER *(blazered, crew-cut, earphoned):* Good afternoon, sports fans, and welcome to another thrilling presentation of the "Sunday Sports Shebang"! I'm Spike Ammidown, your host at this roundup of great sportsmanship, great athletes, and stirring highlights of sports events from around this great globe of ours! Here in the next five hours, you're gonna see, all live, and on tape, too, the ecstasy of victory and the concomitant heartache of defeat, in great climactic scenes of a full dozen major athletic events from the four corners of the earth, brought into your living room by our expert reporters and camera teams, whom you can be sure are standing by at this very minute! Right now, I'm standing here, *live,* on the eighteenth fairway of the Paw-tucket Drive-In Golf-A-Way, where you will see this afternoon the final holes of the great $250,000 Eastern Open Miniature Golf Championship. We'll be bringing those dramatic holes your way in just a few moments, but right now I have a signal from Red Glebman, who is waiting in a front-row seat in our broadcasting booth at Busch Memorial Stadium, in St. Louis, to bring you thrilling action from the final game of the World Series. So come in, Red!

RED GLEBMAN: Thanks, Spike, and good afternoon, ball fans! Here, brought to you *live* from the home of the battlin' Cardinals, we're in the top of the seventh inning of the seventh and final game of the great Fall Classic. The score here is tied up at 0–0 in a real nail-biter, and as you can see in this special shot from our Goodyear blimp high above the Big Muddy, the Tigers have two men on the old basepaths! As the faithful Redbird fans here have learned, these Bengals from the Motor City don't know the meaning of the word "quit." Two out! Two on! Sluggin' Jim Northrup stands in. Bob Gibson, the Redbirds' ace fireballer, has gone all the way, but right now he looks mighty bushed out there. Just *listen* to this crowd! Now he's got the sign. He's taking his stretch! The runners lead away—

SPIKE AMMIDOWN *(back at the Golf-A-Way):* Thanks, Red. And thanks for that magnificent moment from the great world of the national pastime. We'll be getting back to you real soon. Meantime, I have word that Jim Croddy is standing by at the finals of the World Championship Garage Attendants' Parking Rodeo, out in Los Angeles, where he'll be bringing you all that thrilling action *live,* so come on in, Jim!

JIM CRODDY: Thanks a million, Spike, and good afternoon, parking fans! I'm here at the foot of the lower-ramp straightaway of the Acme Minute-Park Garage, in the heart of downtown L.A., where today we'll see the final events of this thrilling Parking Rodeo including the $50,000 Top-Floor-to-Street-Level Compact Car Delivery Sprints, in which the nine finalists, from a Le Mans start, will vie for control of this single steep ramp! Here beside me, *live,* at this moment, is Luther (Ace) Purdy, the defending champion in this event, who is currently in third place in the over-all standings with 12,564,811.49 points. Ace, you dropped back to third yesterday when the judges gave you only 24.41 points on Style at the conclusion of your great run in the Unlimited Class Curved-Ramp Backup. How do you feel about that?

ACE PURDY: Well, Jim, I'm glad you ast me that, because I sure got a raw deal. I mean, I don't want to fault these great judges or nothin', but when that fender fell offn the Jag at the top of the ramp, I didn't have nothin' to do with it a-tall. I mean, when I jumped into that Jag I seen that that fender was just held on there with a little piece of old baling wire or something. One of these crazy rookies musta whanged it off in one of the qualifyin' runs. I'm appealing those Style points to the International Federation. Just see if I don't!

JIM CRODDY: Good for you, Ace! And thanks for those fighting sentiments from a great sporting gentleman!

SPIKE AMMIDOWN (*breaking in again*): Thanks, Jim, for that exciting on-the-spot interview. We have an urgent signal from Red Glebman at Busch Memorial Stadium, which means that things must be popping at that final Series game! We'll get back to Red in just a minute, at the conclusion of this important message from our sponsor.

SPIKE AMMIDOWN: Well, here we are again, fans, with more of your "Sunday Sports Shebang"! Before we get back to Red Glebman, who seems to have some mighty hot news for us— take it easy there, Red, boy!—we want to jump down to Tex Guttweiler, who is standing by, *live,* at the finals of the Panhandle Senior Mixed Doubles Tennis Championships, at the Broomstraw Country Club, in Amarillo. It's all yours, Tex!

TEX GUTTWEILER (*whispering*): Thanks, Spike, and good afternoon, mixed-doubles fans! This *has* to be great timing, because at this moment the finals stand here at match point! Mrs. Eloise MacKittrup and her partner, Bob Spurge, are trailing Mr. and Mrs. Billy-Joe Jenkins, 1–6, 0–5, in this second set. It's love–40 and Mrs. MacKittrup is serving. Right now, things look mighty black for the MacKittrup-Spurge duo, but as everyone down here in the Panhandle knows, they're all heart, and I wouldn't be surprised if we were about to see the beginning of a great fighting comeback. Mrs. MacKittrup is gritting her teeth. She toes the line—here's the serve! Oop—she hit it into the net! It's a fault. Here's the old second serve. Uh-oh—it's *out!* It's a good eight feet out, and this match is over! And there you have it, folks, *live* from Amarillo—the Double Fault of the Week! Back to you, Spike, fella.

SPIKE AMMIDOWN: How *'bout* that, Tex! Thanks for that great on-the-spot coverage. Now, before we go to Red Glebman at the World Series—relax, Red, for crying out loud! It's just a game— we want to bring you a fascinating feature story that I taped in person last week at the village of Izquirra, high in the Basque country of northern Spain, as an exclusive for the "Sunday Sports Shebang." So, without more ado, we'll roll that for you. Over to me, in Izquirra! . . . Good afternoon, folks! It's I, Spike Ammidown, here in the main street of Izquirra, a mighty long way from Pawtucket, from where I'll be showing you this from next Sunday. Such is the wonder of our shrinking, sports-loving globe! Today I'm going to bring you, exclusive and for the first time on any network, the annual championship game of Qub, the national Basque sport that is played only here in Izquirra. As you can see, I am surrounded by the villagers, who are garbing themselves with their interesting equipment and planning team strategy just before the whistle that will start this exciting eight-hour contest. Standing beside me is Raimondo Uzcuden, the Mayor of Izquirra and the only inhabitant who speaks English, who will explain to us some of the fine points of Qub. Tell us, Mayor Uzcuden, how many players are there on a side in Qub?

MAYOR UZCUDEN: Eet depends.

SPIKE AMMIDOWN: I see. And these tall wicker baskets the players are strapping to their heads—what are they called?

MAYOR UZCUDEN: Zhey have no name. Just old baskets.

SPIKE AMMIDOWN: Yes. Now, as I understand it, the players *catch* the ball, or *qub,* in these head-baskets and then dribble or pass the *qub* to their teammates at top speed. And the players must keep their hands in their pockets *at all times.* Is that correct?

MAYOR UZCUDEN: Ees correct.

SPIKE AMMIDOWN: And what is the ball, or *qub,* made of?

MAYOR UZCUDEN: Sometimes ees a stone. Sometimes ees ball of feathers. This year, ees a Coke bottle.

SPIKE AMMIDOWN: Golly! And how are the two goals demarcated?

MAYOR UZCUDEN: Uphill goal ees Don Federico's donkey. Downhill goal ees *bodega* window. Goalie pays eef window gets broken. Keeps heem on toes, no?

SPIKE AMMIDOWN: Thank you, Mayor! *Gracias, amigo!* And there you have it, Qub fans—the ancient rules of this ancient game! We'll be back a little later with some great action scenes of this dangerous and lightning-fast sport, but first here's another message from our sponsor.

SPIKE AMMIDOWN: Here we are, sports lovers, back in the good old U.S.A. and *live* at the Pawtucket Golf-A-Way, all ready with more of your "Sunday Sports Shebang." A few moments ago, we brought you a taped view of some of the complexities of that dangerous Basque game of Qub. Now we know you're ready for simpler, more familiar fare—a game that you all know and love. In short, it's pro football time! Buddy Pitts and his crew are perched high above the fifty-yard line at Memorial Stadium in Ottumwa, Iowa, where the second quarter of the game between the Ottumwa Chiefs and the Hannibal Elephants is in progress. Right after this live report, we'll get back to Red Glebman and the World Series in St. Louis. So take it, Buddy Pitts!

BUDDY PITTS: Thanks, Spike, and good afternoon, grid fans! Here in Ottumwa, the score is tied, 24–24, midway through the second quarter in this rock-'em, sock-'em game between the hard-nosed behemoths of the Des Moines Valley League. There's time out on the field, so I'm gonna ask Pudge Spivack, the great former All-League guard who is our play-spotter, to come in and analyze that last play for you. Pudge?

PUDGE SPIVAK: Thanks, Buddy. Now, as most of you fans must have recognized, that last play was the Two-X Blue-29 Sprint-out Deep Option. As you can see on the blackboard here, Whitey Bamberger takes the snap, fakes to a running back coming across, fakes to the fullback cutting inside, and then rolls out to his right behind the two pulling guards. The center, Sprazzuolo, has to trap the strongside tackle, O'Toole, and the *offensive* strongside tackle, Rudinsky, double-teams the middle line-backer, "Big Mother" Majurciewicz, with Spranghausen, the leading guard. Meantime, the tight end, Krock, takes off with the snap, fakes a right turn-in, then fakes a left zig-out, and *then* runs a straight fly pattern. The wide receiver, Poole, fakes a buttonhook, then actually *does* buttonhook and floats back to take a safety-valve pass if needed. The split end, "Fingers" Guildenschaft, meantime fakes a five-yard loop-out to the right, then cuts back for a little look-in pass over center. On *dee*-fense, the Elephants' corner linebacker, Karakashian, keyed on Krock—unless, of course, Guildenschaft had overshifted, in which case Karakashian's key on Krock collapses the corner covered by Holtzapple, the safety man, who was in tight on the Shirley Red Dog. Of course, on this play Whitey Bamberger dropped the snap from center and had to fall on the ball, so none of this made much difference. O.K., Buddy?

BUDDY PITTS: O.K., Pudge, and thanks. I'm sure all our millions of viewers were glad to have their analysis of that last play clearly confirmed by you. We'll have more football action in just a few minutes, but meantime it's back to Spike Ammidown in Pawtucket. Take it, Coach!

SPIKE AMMIDOWN: Thank you, thank you, Buddy. There's nothing like football for thrills, is there, fans? Well, it's all over at Busch Memorial Stadium, folks. The final game of the 1968 Series is history! Red Glebman is standing by with a recap wrapup of that great chapter of the Fall Classic, but since the game is over, we can wait and hear from Red in just a few minutes. Meantime, here at the Pawtucket Golf-A-Way, I see that the final-round leaders in this $250,000 Eastern Miniature Golf Open are now on the fifteenth tee, so I think I'd better make you all familiar with the layout of this challenging final eighteenth hole. As you can see, this *has* to be a magnificent test, measuring sixty-five feet four inches—one of those truly demanding par 3s. So far in the tourney, there have only been four aces carded here, each entitling the lucky player to another round at no extra charge. From this elevated tee, a long hitter can aim across this narrow, tilted teeter-totter, hoping to drop the ball safely on the other side, beyond the Enchanted Forest, and then straight into the Gnome's open mouth—a shot that will come out the pipe on the other side of Toad Hall and right onto the old green. *Or*, if he's a little weak off the tee, he can play it safe by fading his drive up this little garden path, between the rows of cockleshells, past the rotating vanes of Little Bopeep's windmill—which takes cool, cool timing, believe you me—and then over London Bridge and onto the green. Even if his shot fades too much, which is possible today in this left-to-right wind, and goes off the bridge, there's just a *chance* that the ball will hit one of these little concrete lily pads and—

But now I see it's time for our stations to identify themselves, so I'll let them come in now and, uh, identify themselves from coast to coast. Now, don't forget to stay right with us, sports fans, because we have plenty more action to bring your way this afternoon. We'll have further *live* coverage from all those great events you've already seen, including good old Red Glebman's on-the-spot summary of that big seventh game of the World Series. And, above and beyond all this, we'll bring you a special report, relayed to you *live* by Pacific Telstar, on the Two Million Metre Himalayan Walkathon, straight from Darjeeling; the Prep School Touch Football Play of the Week, taped at yesterday's Donnybrook between the Seniors and Upper Middlers at Governor Dummer; water-skiing grandmothers at Lake Tahoe; and lots, *lots* more! So don't go 'way, sports fans. Stay right there in your seats and get ready for more healthful, thrilling moments on your "Sunday Sports Shebang"!

Keeping Up
with the Outs

CLUB'S DÉBUT SEPARATES THE INS FROM THE OUTS
It wasn't easy to find Arthur at Arthur Wednesday night, but everyone else was there—Caterine and D.D. and Jane, Jake and Mike and Rudolf, all those "in" people who know that Arthur is a place and not a person.
—*Angela Taylor in* The New York Times

One of the people who didn't know that Arthur is a place and not a person is Mrs. Herbert W. Spangenberg of Leonia, N.J., who almost missed the news altogether. As it was, she caught up with the fact that Arthur is the name of Sybil Burton's new discothèque three days late, and, as she said later, it was the funniest thing that she noticed it at all. She was out in the hall late Sunday night just flopping down this big bunch of newspapers on top of the two trash baskets and the garbage pail and the three full wastebaskets—it's *something* the way the papers and trash pile up at the Spangenbergs' over the weekend, especially if they have friends in for supper on Friday or Saturday night, or if young Herbert, Jr. (who is known as Hub), is home on pass from Fort Belvoir—when her eye was caught by this flash of a headline that began with the name "Arthur." Well, as she told Mr. Spangenberg a few minutes later, and as she explained more fully the next morning in a telephone call to her friend Janet Mulleavy (Mrs. Francis T. Mulleavy, of 31-09 Two Hundred and Fourteenth Place), she had just been trying to flump the newspapers into any sort of a pile that wouldn't fall off the trash cans and onto the floor and make Angelo, the super, sore in the morning, and she had been holding the apartment door open with one foot and trying at the same time to keep Bingo, the Spangenbergs' Boston bull, from coming out into the hall; but after that glimpse of the word "Arthur" she pressed the little button on the door that releases the lock, and then closed the door, thus confining Bingo, and then went back and riffled through all the papers right there in the hall until she found the story in the old Friday *Times* with the headline, "ARTHUR, ONCE A HAIRDO, IS NOW A DISCOTHÈQUE." The really funny thing about it all, as she told Herb and, later on, Janet, is that she doesn't care much one way or the other about discothèques, but she always sort of pricks up her ears when she sees the word "Arthur," and that's because "Arthur" to her means her brother, of course—Arthur Briscoe, of Canandaigua, N.Y. Not that Art Briscoe gets in the paper very often, or anything like that. He is eleven years older than Mrs. Spangenberg (she was Florence Briscoe before she went to Cornell on a Regents' scholarship in the fall of 1936; she dropped out after that one year and married Herb Spangenberg, who was a senior and a Kappa Sig), and five years ago Art retired after forty-one years with Northern Mohawk Power and Light. Florence and her brother have sort of lost touch with each other over the years, though they always exchange Christmas presents, and last year the Briscoes came to town over Washington's Birthday, staying at the Spangenbergs' for three whole days. But Florence cares about Arthur, and that's why she always looks twice when she sees an Arthur in the papers because it might be Art. Oh, not an obituary—Florence isn't gloomy that way, even though Art is in his sixties now—but you never can tell. And there was that time back in 1948 when Florence did find Arthur's name in the paper—his name *and* his picture—when he was an alternate delegate to the Republican National Convention, which was held in Philadelphia. Nobody in the New York delegation got sick or anything, so Art didn't get to vote for Governor Dewey at the convention, but Florence still has the clipping somewhere, and probably that's how she got the habit of noticing the name Arthur in the newspapers.

Florence Spangenberg read the *Times* story about the discothèque named Arthur right through while standing out in the hall in her green polka-dot cotton bathrobe, and then she tore out the story and headline, and after pushing the other button that reset the front-door lock and shushing Bingo, who had begun to bark when she came back in, she took the clipping into the bedroom and told Herb about how funny it was, her mistaking a new discothèque for her brother. Herb was in bed, almost asleep but trying to watch a Bob Hope movie called *Paris Holiday* on the Late Show, because Anita Ekberg was in it, and he listened to Florence, nodding his head to show her he was paying attention but really watching the TV screen, but when his wife began to read the clipping aloud he said, "Oh, what *is* all this, Flo, for Christ's sake, anyway?" and she stopped. But the next morning, after Herb had gone to work, she called Janet, and Janet agreed that it was really peculiar learning about the discothèque named Arthur in that funny way. Janet Mulleavy then added that she wondered how Florence could have missed knowing about Arthur for all this time, because it had been in all the columns for months and months now, and people were always talking about it on the Johnny Carson Show, because it was *the* place to go, as all the "in" people knew. "Well," Florence Spangenberg said, "I just didn't see it anywhere before last night out in the hall. I guess I must be getting old, or something, but I didn't see anything about it." Pretty soon she hung up. Her feelings were hurt.

•

A fleet of limousines and buses hauled an adequately star-studded cargo of partygoers to a Staten Island country house last night for a supper dance in an elegant pink-and-white striped tent. Trumbull Barton and John L. McHugh gave the gathering in honor of their old friend Dame Margot Fonteyn.

. . . the list also included Mrs. René Bouché, Mr. and Mrs. William Colleran (Lee Remick), Mr. and Mrs. Martin Gabel (Arlene Francis), Alan Jay Lerner and Oliver Messel, Lord Snowdon's uncle. The Livingston Biddles had declined, and Mr. Blass sent his regrets. Truman Capote, on the other hand, did not answer his invitation.

—*Charlotte Curtis, in* The New York Times

Another person who didn't turn up at the Trumbull Barton–John L. McHugh party for Dame Margot Fonteyn is Owen Sperry, thirty-nine, of 18 East Eleventh Street. If Mr. Sperry hadn't been in bed with the flu and a temperature of just over a hundred and one, he probably wouldn't have known about the party at all, because he doesn't usually get around to the society and women's pages in the *Times*, but that morning (it was a Tuesday), after he had called his secretary and told her again that he wouldn't be in and explained that the doctor had said that there was nothing to do for these things but stay in bed and take aspirin and drink lots of water and wait it out, sometimes for as long as ten days, he hung up, and then, with his head propped up on three pillows, he read his way languidly and slowly through the *Times*, occasionally falling into a light doze and then waking and going on with the paper. He found the story about the supper dance and read it all the way through—almost a column and a half—and it occurred to him that it was the first time he had ever come upon a social report that ended with a list of absentees. He tossed the *Times* on the floor, poured himself another glass of water and made himself drink it, and lay back and closed his eyes, and in his mind he composed what seemed to be a logical continuation to the story: ". . . Truman Capote, on the other hand, did not answer his invitation. Curiously, Mr. and Mrs. Owen Sperry (Adelaide Jencks) received no invitation to the party in the first place, and neither did Miss Linda Sperry, 12, the student. Reached late last night, Mr. Sperry stated that he certainly would have acknowledged the invitation, one way or the other, had it appeared in the Sperry mailbox. The list of the uninvited also included Mrs. Howard Jencks, of Pelham, who is Miss Sperry's grandmother, Dr. Leonard Farbson, the dedicated influenza fighter, Peter D. Falkenhausen, who is Mr. Sperry's employer, and—" Here Sperry, who was undoubtedly feeling his fever, decided to go on and make a mental list of everyone he knew who could not possibly have been at the party. Luckily, he had only gone through a dozen-odd names when he got stuck trying to remember the name of the old lady who had lived with three Pomeranians on the ground floor of the Sperry's old apartment on Christopher Street (she never would have left the dogs to go way out to Staten Island for a supper dance), and the effort of thinking back and muttering "Matthews? ... Marx? ... Mameluke?" soon put him to sleep once again.

By afternoon, Sperry had forgotten about the Barton-Mc-Hugh party. He tried to do a little manuscript reading in bed (Mr. Sperry is an editor with a small, conservative, and not very successful publishing house), but he couldn't pay attention, and he put in a couple of hours dazedly watching quiz programs on the TV set. A little after four, Linda Sperry came home from school. She inspected him from the doorway through her horn-rimmed glasses and announced, "Boy, you look *terrible*." Pretty soon, Mrs. Sperry came home from her job at the uptown girls' school where she teaches remedial reading, and set about neatening up the sickroom. Owen Sperry got up and shaved while his wife remade the bed with fresh sheets, and then he changed into clean pajamas and climbed back into bed. He felt a little better, and there were some branches of new lilacs in a vase on his bureau. Later, he ate a light supper of cold madrilène and aspirin. That evening, his wife read aloud to him—a couple of chapters from an old Evelyn Waugh novel—and by ten-fifteen he was asleep, with the lights out and the door closed.

For the past three or four years, however, Owen Sperry had been bothered with insomnia—not the kind that keeps you from falling asleep but the kind that nudges you awake sometime between four and six in the morning—and on this night he awoke again long before first light. He lay there in the dark, his pajama collar damp with sweat, and muzzily cursed the ineffectual sleeping pill he had taken. In recent months, Sperry's night thoughts have been of a singularly depressing nature—cancer, flash fires, automobile collisions, his lack of progress in his office, recent cruelties and stupidities of his own making—but this time something made him remember the elegant party he had read about in the *Times*. In the dark, in the middle of the night, he felt bitter about it, instead of amused, and he finally said aloud, "Well, why *weren't* we invited?" He didn't know the hosts, that was why, and after a little reflection he realized that he probably wouldn't have known one guest there, either. He didn't know any real celebrities—only a couple of moderately acclaimed authors. Once, when he was fourteen, he had played ping-pong with Fay Wray at a resort hotel in New Hampshire. He and his wife would have had a lousy time at that party; they would have been stuck with each other in a corner, trying to make conversation and pretending they didn't care. And he had just about forgotten how to dance. Oh, it wasn't himself and his wife he cared about so much; it was Linda. When he was in college, he had gone to some pretty nifty débutante parties, but he and Adelaide hadn't kept up with that sort of world after their marriage. They weren't much for parties. But now he had to face it: there was a pretty good chance that Linda would never get to go to a supper dance by limousine. His fault. He lay there and saw Linda—Linda grown up but looking the same, with her brown hair and her glasses and her plump arms—standing unnoticed outside a pink-and-white striped tent, with music coming through the night trees. Next thing he knew, he was crying.

Sperry has had enough experience with night thoughts to know that the thing to do is get out of bed, turn on the lights, find a snack—anything to break the chain. Out of habit, he now got up and fumbled for his bathrobe in the dark, even though his wife was sleeping in the study during his sickness and wouldn't have been awakened if he had just stayed there in bed and read a book for a while. He found an old quilt and wrapped it around his shoulders and then went down to the dark hall and into the living room. He flicked on the lights, picked up some magazines from the stack on the coffee table, and sat down in the wing chair, tucking the quilt around his feet. It was strange being in the living room for the first time in so long. Over by the window, his wife's house plants looked different, as if he had surprised them in the night. Then Sperry heard creaking and footsteps, and his wife came into the room. She was barefoot, wearing just her nightgown, and her arms were crossed in front of her. Her eyes were blinking in the light.

"What on *earth?*" she said. "What are you doing up? I heard you banging around."

"Couldn't sleep," Sperry explained. "You know how I get."

"But you're sick." She leaned over and felt his forehead. "Listen," she said, "as long as you're all covered up here, just sit tight and I'll take your temperature again."

She went out, and when she came back she was wearing her bathrobe and shaking down the thermometer. She stuck it in his mouth and sat on the arm of the next chair and waited. Even with the sleepy, concerned expression on her face and the hair clips over her ears, she looked pretty to him. It was something special, the two of them being in the living room in the middle of the night.

She took the thermometer back. "Only ninety-nine two," she said. "And now back to bed with you. I think you're getting better."

"I do, too," said Owen Sperry. He followed her down the hall, trailing his quilt. She straightened the rumpled bed once again, and he climbed in. He wanted to tell her that he had been crying because of a story in the *Times* about a big party on Staten Island, but the minute he got into bed he was overcome with sleepiness, and it seemed too complicated to explain. He would tell her in the morning, if he remembered. She turned out the lights, and Sperry went right to sleep.

Brush Twice Daily and Go Easy on the Bonbons

I was at my dentist's. I should have been relaxed, because it was only a cleaning and checkup, but I was suffering from a small, undeserved hangover, and the injustice of this made me edgy. I squirmed in the chair, trying to get comfortable, and closed my eyes against the bright nine-o'clock sun. My head pounded dully, and each scrape of the doctor's metal pick on my lower right molars reverberated unpleasantly in some deep interior echo chamber. My head was a cave, full of noisy spelunkers. I stirred, and the doctor's instrument pricked my gum.

"Hey!" I said. "Watch it."

"Oh-oh," said my dentist. " 'Fraid I made a booboo."

He squirted the gum, and I rinsed and spat. "God," I muttered under my breath. " 'Booboo.' 'Oh-oh.' "

The dentist glanced at me sharply through his rimless half-glasses and then turned and selected another pick. "Sorry," he said, scraping again, "but it's hard not to make a booboo when I'm getting off tartar."

For some reason, I was suddenly on guard. I tried to gauge the man, but the sun, bouncing off his spectacles, hid his eyes in an impenetrable dazzle. I decided to test him.

"How are my gums?" I said when he next straightened up. "Any signs of beriberi?"

"Just so-so," he replied, turning his back. "They'd be better if you'd massage them. I recommend two toothbrushes."

"Two toothbrushes!" I cried. "Here, here, you've gone too far."

"Sorry," he said pushing me gently back in the chair. "That was a bit rococo, I admit. A barbarity."

"Oh, I wouldn't say *that*," I said magnanimously.

"Yes, you would," he said, scraping on my uppers now, "if you thought about it."

I thought about it, and ground my half-cleaned teeth. Then I made myself lie back. I cogitated furiously, planning my attack. My headache was gone, and my mind raced ahead like some gigantic, avenging hound. The dentist was polishing now, but his concentration seemed uncertain, and I thought his hand trembled for a moment. It came to me that he was holding my jaw open in sheer self-defense.

Suddenly he turned off the humming brush. "Did you murmur?" he asked in a kindly voice.

"No!" I shouted. "I mean, uh, yes. I was only going to say that beriberi is less common among the Mau Maus than sleeping sickness, which is caused, of course, by tsetse flies."

"No doubt. Whereas Berbers sustain healthy gums on a day-to-day diet of pawpaws and couscous. Among the Shoshones—"

"Nothing else?" I said hastily. "No condiments? Not even chowchow?"

"Not even jujubes," he said. "Though they sometimes hunt the Persian songbird, or bulbul, which they bring down with dumdums and then bake into a savory pie, as delicious to them as is a baba au rhum to Coco Chanel."

"Yum-yum," I muttered faintly.

"Once, from a small put-put on Lake Titicaca—"

"Can't we leave these damn foreign countries you know so much about?" I snapped. "All those copies of *National Geographic* you get for your waiting room . . . It isn't *fair!*"

"Aye, aye, sir!" he replied at once, swinging the X-ray machine over my head. "Done and done! Let our causerie range, taking in the world *in toto*. What'll it be—show biz? Sports? Art, with its Neo-Dada trend? Or the more chichi world of the yé-yé set? We aren't old dodoes yet, are we?"

"Baseball!" I cried. "That pitcher, Bobo Newsom—"

"Was a lulu," he said heartily, inserting the X-ray film clamp between my teeth. "As were Jo-Jo Moore and Choochoo Coleman. And let us not overlook Kiki Cuyler. As Papa Hemingway once observed, Kiki was the Gogol of the—"

"Enough baseball!"

"Tut-tut, don't upset yourself. On to Broadway, then—the thespians. Why, only last week I saw Zizi Jeanmaire, Mimi Hines, Dede Allen, and Bibi Osterwald dining together at Zum Zum. Zizi sans tutu, natch. Lovely ladies! Admirable masticators! But no prettier, I must admit, than were Fifi Dorsay and Anna Sten, the go-go girls of an earlier camera era. I used to make goo-goo eyes at Fifi."

"But Anna Sten—" I began.

"Starred in *Nana*," he said softly. "Or were you thinking of the Sten gun, a pom-pom used in World War II?"

The X-ray clicked for the last time, and the dentist removed the plate and whisked the cloth from my neck. Only then did he notice my tears, my heaving shoulders.

"Come, come!" he said, patting my arm in a friendly way. "Cheer up. No cavities! There is nothing to fear."

My sobs grew louder. "Gub-Gub!" I wailed. "Gub-Gub. Dab-Dab."

"Pull yourself together, man," he said, peering anxiously at me. "I fear our little chin-chin has deranged you. You sound coo-coo."

"No," I whispered, snuffling. "I just remembered about Gub-Gub and Dab-Dab. Those animals in *Doctor Do-hoo-hoo* . . . In *Doctor Dolittle*. Gub-Gub the pig and Dab-Dab the duck. I used to love them so when I was a little bu-huh-huh . . . when I was a little boy. And then they went and put them into that awful m-movie with Rex Harrison. Oh, I wish they'd left my little animals alone!"

"To which I cry a hearty hear-hear!" said the doctor. "I much preferred the animals in *Lili* and the songs in *Gigi*." He dried my face with the cloth, straightened my tie, and then put his arm around my shoulders and helped me to my feet. While I attempted to collect myself, he rummaged in a box of lollipops and small toys he keeps for his younger patients and then pressed something into my hand. "Here," he said softly, "this is for you."

It was a Yo-Yo.

"Gee, thank you, Dcotor," I said, delighted with my prize. "And I'll see you in six months."

He took me to the door and waved cheerily as I started down the hall. "Bye-bye," he said.

Life in These
Now United States

(The *Reader's Digest* Is Captured by the Enemy)

America Grooves

Officer Bob, who has directed traffic on our Main Street for as long as most of us can remember, saw a long-haired, typically "messy-looking" youth crossing against the lights one morning. He blew his whistle, stopping all traffic, and said, "Watch your step, Miss." When the teen-ager glared at him, the well-liked minion of the law smiled and said, "Oh, I beg your pardon. I thought you were a girl. You *look* like a girl."

"And you look like J. Edgar Hoover's grandmother in drag," shot back the youngster. He stepped closer to Officer Bob and said, "Listen, Fuzzhead, if you read anything besides *The Spanker's Monthly*, you'd know by now that hostility to unusual forms of male dress almost invariably conceals a repressed homosexuality, marked by hysteria and frequent episodes of enraged brutality. Likewise, if you could stop fondling the butt of the Smith & Wesson Police Special like some cornball Rod Steiger, you might notice that you've been wising off at the son of the First Selectman. My pop has his eye on you, *Sturmbannführer*, and you'd better, like, get on the stick."

The next morning, when the same young man appeared at Officer Bob's crossing, they had a briefer exchange. "Pig!" said the lad. "Punk!" muttered Officer Bob. That day, however, Officer Bob gave out forty-seven tickets for overtime parking, issued fourteen summonses to schoolchildren for loitering, and arrested an eighty-three-year-old grandmother for driving with a mud-spattered license plate. Now he is our town's Chief of Police. "I sure learned my lesson," says Officer Bob, twinkling. "The kids are where it's at."—Betty Birch (in the Iowa *Grunt*).

•

In addition to her duties as our school-bus driver and town clerk, my Great-Aunt Hannah, a widow, is a nudist. Every afternoon, rain or shine, she lies down on the glider on her front porch, as naked as a doorknob (see "Toward a More With-It Speech," p. 89.—*Ed.*), and reads *Sunshine and Health*, in plain view of all the traffic on Elm Street. As you can imagine, this has caused some "talk," but over the years our town has learned to put up with her little ways. "If we just ignore her," said the Rev. Gantry, the Jansenist minister, "maybe she'll knock it off. Or catch a bad cold," he added, chuckling.

Last fall, Aunt Hannah's granddaughter, Esther-Mae, went off to college at State U., and a few weeks later Esther-Mae's picture appeared on the front page of the new undergraduate paper there; she was taking part in a Grape Strike Pageant, and she was as naked as a darning egg. (Very good!—*Ed.*) Now Esther-Mae has moved to the East Village, in New York, where we hear she has embarked on a profitable film career, and lots of the kids in our town have taken to spending the afternoons with Great-Aunt Hannah on the porch, where they eat cookies and look at her picture books. As my husband says, "It only shows to go you—you can't knock tolerance!"—Alice Leonowens (from *The Pharmacist's Retort*).

Freaking Out Loud

I've discovered what's bugging my Dad—the F.B.I.!—Buddy Fliegelman, in the P.S. 92 *Grab-Bag*.

Marriage is a long sentence that begins with a proposition.— *The Christian Dentist*.

We had a prairie fire last summer, and by the time it was over the whole town was smoking grass. Get it?—Tom Beeber (Petunia, Colo.).

I can read my Dad like a book—and he wears a plain brown wrapper.—Buddy Fliegelman, *op. cit.*

A Boy Named Ernesto

Another Boring Story from Everyday Life

One afternoon, many years ago, a rich American was having his shoes shined on a sidewalk in Cienfuegos, a city in Cuba. The ragged local boy on his knees before him was working away with a will, humming a native song and making the shoecloth pop. The American removed his Panama hat and wiped the perspiration from his brow with a silk handkerchief, and then puffed with satisfaction on his Havana cigar. It had been a good day for him. He was a broker for the United Fruit Company, and that morning he had concluded a profitable deal with a corrupt landowner that would halve the wages for several thousand local sugar-workers while simultaneously depriving them of their right ever to own bicycles. He had also arranged with the wily governor of the province to raise the tax on literacy—a plan that would swell the already bloated coffers of the infamous United Fruit monopoly. Yes indeedy, it was a good day!

The boy finished his labors, and the American handed him a counterfeit peso.

"No teep, señor?" asked the lad, with an impudent grin.

"No 'teep,' Pedro," said the man, tousling his hair. "Sorry 'bout that. The sooner you greaseballs learn to stand on your own feet and give an honest day's work for an honest day's pay, the sooner us gringos will be hotfooting it to Switzerland with the last contents of your Treasury. *Comprende?*"

"*Si, señor,*" piped the boy. "And *muchas gracias* for another valuable lesson in laissez-faire economics. I won't be needing your filthy lagniappe any more, for I'm off for the Sierra Maestra." And he threw the lead coin in the man's face and strode away.

Only then did the American glance down and notice that the peasant lad had shined his nice white shoes with stove polish. He started after him with an oath, but the clever youngster had tied his shoelaces together, and the imperialist fell heavily to the pavement and fractured his pince-nez.

"*Ay, Chihuahua!*" cried the boy's mother, who had been watching this scene from the window of her slum. "Ernesto, come back! We will starve—and besides, you have forgotten to brush your teeth *con* Gleem!"

"I will be back, *Mamacita,* astride the wind of history!" cried the boy from the corner. "One day—I swear it to you, *madre mia*—this man's son will pin my likeness, in a giant poster, to the wall of his room at the Groton School!"

The ragged boy was right. Che Guevara was on his way!

Put-Ons: The Best Medicine

One evening last autumn, second graders at the Vapid Falls, Minnesota, elementary school locked their principal, Mr. Forbush, in a mop closet and proceeded to wreck his office. They burned the school records and stuffed Mallomars into his dictating machine. They poured ink all over his checkbook, mucilage in his rubbers, and raspberry Kool-Aid in his box of cigars. They tore down his picture of President Harding and played kickball with his globe.

The next morning, after the school janitor had released him from the mop closet, Forbush went directly to the second-grade room. "O.K., kids," he said to the class. "I'm ready to talk turkey. Amnesty for demonstrators is guaranteed. Compulsory naps are abolished. What are your demands?"

The boys and girls looked at each other in astonishment. "What demands, Mr. Forbush?" piped up Billy Fraser at last. "Gee whiz, haven't you ever heard of Trick or Treat?"

"Holy mackerel, I forgot about Halloween!" Forbush cried, smacking himself on the forehead and laughing heartily. "The joke's on me, kids." Still chuckling, he expelled the entire class.

•

Hiram Warsaw, a nineteen-year-old Bronx dropout, grew tired of making obscene telephone calls one day. Instead, he looked up the name of the last man in the Manhattan telephone book and called him up. "Hello, Mr. Zzyzybyzynsky?" he said.

"Yes?" said Mr. Zzyzybyzynsky warily.

"I was just looking in the phone book and I noticed—"

"Yeah, I know, I *know!*" Mr. Zzyzybyzynsky shouted.

"Don't hang up!" Warsaw said. "Listen, I just saw you were the last name in the phone book and I thought I'd call you up, because my name is Aababonowicz and I'm the *first* man in the Manhattan book."

"No kidding?" said Zzyzybyzynsky, interested.

"Yeah, how *about* that!" Warsaw said. "I was thinking we ought to get together somewhere, Mr. Zzyzybyzynsky, and rap about our problems. I mean, we have a lot in common."

"Yeah, O.K., sure thing," said Mr. Zzyzybyzynsky eagerly. "Where shall we meet?"

"Oh, around the 'Ms' somewhere," said Warsaw, and hung up. The next day, in an inexplicable fit of ennui, he enlisted in the Marines for a four-year hitch.

New Hope for Lycanthropy

Thanks to the Treatment of a Courageous Backwoods Psychiatrist, Victims of America's Most Whispered-About Illness Are at Last Taking Their Places in Normal Society.

[*Condensed from* The Garageman's Almanac]

When Ralph Waldo Lupus, the only child of a wealthy Winnetka, Illinois, couple, was about six months old, his mother first noticed that he had long gray hair growing on his palms, but the family pediatrician assured her (wrongly) that this minor oddity would soon "clear itself up." Little Ralph Waldo's boyhood was happy and unnotable—with one exception. Approximately once a month, at the time of the full moon, he would have no appetite for his breakfast. Questioned by Mrs. Lupus, he invariably reported that he felt "full"—rather as if he had eaten several large hamburgers, cooked very rare, during the night. He also told about experiencing vivid dreams of running about the countryside "dressed up like a big doggy." His mother decided he had been reading too many comic books, and thereafter "cracked down" on his reading matter.

For some years, life went along smoothly enough for this typical American family. The only cloud on the Lupuses' horizon was the curious fact that they seemed unable to keep any dogs or other pets on their estate. A series of watchdogs—an Airedale, three dachshunds, a bull terrier, and a large German shepherd—vanished, one by one, after a week or two in residence, always apparently running away during the night. At the same time, Mr. Lupus noted the gradual dwindling of his herd of angora rabbits. One morning, after the hired man had reported the theft or flight of the family's prize Merino ram, young Ralph Waldo, now fourteen, slept very late and then breakfasted on four Alka-Seltzers. Mr. Lupus, pleading a sudden business engagement, packed a bag and hurriedly left the house, never to return.

Alone, and by now deeply concerned about her son's appearance, which seemed to alternate rapidly between emaciation and sleek good health, Mrs. Lupus began a six-year medical odyssey to find diagnosis and treatment for her boy. Across the land, diagnosticians, psychiatrists, dentists, and nutritionists examined Ralph Waldo, and, noting only an unusually rangy musculature of the lower body, pronounced him healthy and normal. At last, depleted in spirit and pocketbook, Mrs. Lupus brought her son last year to the rustic clinic of psychiatrist Dr. Jakob Pretorius, in northern Manitoba. Dr. Pretorius, a small, white-haired man with extremely thick glasses, examined Ralph Waldo for an hour and then sat down for a private chat with Mrs. Lupus.

"Madam," he said bluntly, "I know what you suspect."

"You do?" said Mrs. Lupus, blenching.

"You believe your son to be a victim of lycanthropy. In plain words, you think he is a werewolf."

Mrs. Lupus nodded, her face suffused with shame. "At last, it's out in the open," she murmured.

"Which is half the battle," said the good doctor. "Madam, I can help your son. I can even guarantee a cure. The fact is, Mrs. L., *there is no such thing as lycanthropy!* It exists only in the mind."

"But, Doctor—those howls in the night? Those scrabbling footsteps on the porch roof?"

"Only the wind," said Dr. Pretorius.

"Those sudden changes in appearance?"

"Psychosomatic. You see, your son *believes* he is a werewolf, and so, secretly, do you. You are both victims of a delusion more common than is suspected. Why, *why* must we still go on whispering about lycanthropy! When will we rid ourselves once and for all of this burden of superstition and fear that has come down to us from the Dark Ages? Madam, this is the twentieth century!"

Dr. Pretorius sent Mrs. Lupus back to Winnetka on the next train, having explained that he would lock himself alone in a small room with Ralph Waldo on the night of the next full moon, which was to fall two days later, and then merely awaken the young man at the proper time for "a good, long talk."

A week later, Ralph Waldo Lupus came home, a changed man. There was a new confidence in his step, a ruddy flush of health in his cheeks. Indeed, he seemed so well, so mature, that Mrs. Lupus quickly agreed when he asserted that he wished to seek his fortune in Chicago.

Unfortunately, Mrs. Lupus was not able to thank Dr. Pretorius. His associates have told her that he disappeared on the very night of Ralph Waldo's cure, leaving only his shoes, notebook, and worry beads in the room. They believe him to be suffering from amnesia, brought on by overwork. It is sad he can't see Ralph Waldo Lupus today—a fine young man snatched back by intelligent psychotherapy from a social stigma that now, thanks to Dr. Jakob Pretorius, will be rooted from the darkest places of the American unconscious. Mrs. Lupus visited her son recently and noted with pride that he had gained fifteen pounds and two inches in the past six months. He is a rookie in the Chicago Police

Department, assigned to park patrol, and expects promotion
shortly.

•

Coming Next Month:
Black Power: The Miracle of the Electric Eel
Playin' My Axe: Harold Stassen's New Career as a Rock Musician
Let's Get in God's Bag
From Pot to Hash: Confessions of a Short-Order Cook
Human Encounter Groups: New Hope for the Post Office?
The Friendly Lepers of Katmandu
Getting Busted: The Truth About Those Silicone Treatments
And other articles of heartening credulousness!

Greetings, Friends!

(1986)

Look, friends, before you—can't you see?
Here stands an ancient Christmas tree,
Two columns wide, five decades tall,
On which by custom we install
A chain of names in light suspension,
With tilted rhymes and odd declension,
To please some folks whom we wish well
On the occasion of Noël.
Come on, good reader—let's hang out
And strew these tinsel tunes about
And find some shiny, well-worn rhyme
To couple with "at Christmastime,"
So from this tree may joy descend
On nearest kin and farthest friend
As Yuletide greetings here are sent
To you, our chiefest ornament.
Cheers, my dears! Let blessings rain
On Tina Howe and Michael Caine,
And seasonal bliss drench chaps below,
Like Laurence Tisch, Sebastian Coe,
And further benisons accrue to
Tip O'Neill and Bishop Tutu.
At this season, may we hail
Folks like Dr. Robert Gale,
Hector Babenco, Hayden Carruth,
Father Jenco, and Dr. Ruth?

And while we're hailing, fellows, let's
Hear it for the New York Mets!
Happy Christmas, Julian Lennon!
Joy to Mr. Justice Brennan.
Jimmy Breslin, greet the Day
With Dr. Luc Montagnier,
Molly Ringwald, Mike the Dog,
Tom Hanks, and Michael Lindsay-Hogg.
Hello, North Pole—it's your big night:
Gnomes, prepare the crew for flight,
Get the old gent out of bed,
Hitch up the beasts, unpark the sled.
All set, Kringle? Hit the sky
And rush these gifts to Northrop Frye,
Spalding Gray, Judge Whitman Knapp,
Jam Master Jay, and Laszlo Papp.
Along your way, shake sleigh-borne bells
To titillate the Claiborne Pells;
Then, pack in hand, descend the flue
To stuff the socks of Vida Blue,
Jackie Collins, World B. Free,
Jacques Chirac, and Ming Cho Lee—
Not forgetting that you'll need a
Candy cane for Bob Ojeda,
And matching jammies, just for fun,
For Senator and Trevor Nunn,
And silky nothings to appease
Vanna White and Nan Talese.
In fancy, friends, let's rise and go
By motor through the morning snow
Aboard our Phantom II coupé
To visit friends on Christmas Day—
With gifts and wine and loud rejoicing
We'll wrap up warm and start Rolls-Roycing!
Yo, gents and ladies, cram aboard
And we'll go wake up Richard Ford,
Richard Lugar, Dennis Lamp,

And John Cougar Mellencamp.
Here in the boot there's Veuve Clicquot
For Kenzo and Kirk Varnedoe,
And in the hamper stuff to gladden
Oprah Winfrey and John Madden—
But first I think we should drop off
This goose for Brandon Tartikoff,
And leave the wreaths for Balcomb Greene
And Demi Moore and Geoffrey Beene.
We'll honk the horn in friendly fash
Outside the dorm of Kellye Cash,
And add a boop here by the stoop
Of Surgeon Gen. C. Everett Koop.
What a party! What a gas!
Just call me Mr. Wenceslas!
Clear the street! We've cleared the cupboard
For Buddy Rich and Freddie Hubbard,
Molissa Fenley, Gene Hackman,
Helen Suzman, Wally Backman,
Ken O'Brien, Martin Ritt,
Nolan Ryan, and Benno Schmidt.
Such errands done, we'll chug home, dears,
To pass around the cup that cheers,
And, kith-encircled, cast our gaze
On this humongous Yuley blaze:
Forgathered at the festive hearth
With Judy Woodruff and John Barth,
We'll let our carollings propel
Happiness to Blaine Littell.
With kindly thoughts we'll dwell upon
The likes of Smokey Robinson,
Alice Walker, Judy Pfaff,
Jonathan Demme, Steffi Graf,
Matilda Cuomo, Anne Yarowsky,
Representative Rostenkowski;
And ask that Christmas bless by turns
John Cage and James MacGregor Burns,

Zippy the Pinhead, Benjamin Ward,
Helga, MOMA, Harrison Ford,
Sting, the Spocks (Doc and Mr.),
Julia Child, and Twisted Sister,
Columbia foot- and Lucille Ball,
Bartles & Jaymes, and Carnegie Hall!

Old dreams at Christmas that come creeping
We give to children for safekeeping:
Peace to all men, peace to nations
Light our brief, sweet celebrations.
Friend, arise at Christmas mildish
And pray the days make us more childish,
And peace at last become the reason
Our hopes stay green in every season.

Greetings, Friends!

(1989)

Hark the chime! The year is fleeting—
Time to start our annual meeting!
Sentient readers, would you try
Envisioning this page a pie:
Some deep-dish metaphoric mince
Your bard's concocted to evince
A taste of bygone Christmastimes,
With gentle thoughts and childish rhymes
And thrown-in carollings as well,
And homily and doggerel,
Which serve to say, when all is done,
God rest you, neighbors, every one!
Now bliss befall us, star or cipher:
Happy Christmas, Michelle Pfeiffer!
Barbara Boxer, joy on you, too;
Hail, ye Bosox, Archibishop Tutu!
Pax vobiscum, Sting, and *pax* on
Alan King, LaToya Jackson,
C. Ev'rett Koop, Lovely Billups,
Quincy Troupe, and Jayne Ann Phillips.
Come, choirboys, in *canzoni* loose a
Joyful noise for Tony LaRussa,
And further melodies in praise
Of Wolfgang Puck and Dottie Hayes;
And songs at dawn (a touch *aubade*-sy)

For such as Eduard Shevardnadze,
Then cooler strains, all David Byrne-y,
For Michael Frayn and A. R. Gurney,
Mr. Goodwrench, Freeman Dyson,
Judi Dench, and Michael Tyson!
May I avert at this sweet time
To certain favored friends of mine?
Of Nam June Paik I've found I'm fond;
I think the world of Greg LeMond.
Mookie Wilson! Nicolas Cage!
At my place, guys, you're all the rage.
I feel benevolence, what's more,
For Easy Goer and Albert Gore,
And trust a gladsome Yuley glow
Enfolds Bill White and Phoebe Snow,
And wish, within this Christmas card,
Delicious things for Molly Yard,
And brighter days some folks could use
In Charleston and in Santa Cruz.
Let's hear more toasts in Yule collations
For types in lively occupations,
Like Andrew Young, the doughty mayor,
Or Radu Lupu, Schubert player;
Chuck Jones, the wily Looney Tuner;
Malcolm Forbes, high-style ballooner;
Roger Kingdom, who's a sprinter;
Plus a playwright, Harold Pinter;
Penn Jillette, that glib Houdini;
Gabriela Sabatini
And Michael Chang (tennis twofer);
Sunday Silence, well-paid hoofer;
Margaret Thatcher, premier Brit;
And Blue Jay catcher Ernie Whitt.
Hey, Santa, startle in their p.j.s
R. J. Lurtsema, prince of d.j.s,
Donna Karan, Simon Schama,

Amy Tan, and the Dalai Lama.
Frequent fliers! Midnight hearties!
Hop aboard our Christmas parties:
With David Lodge and David Hare
We'll host a bash in Delaware,
And thence to Pensacola travel
With Glynis Johns and Václav Havel,
Or stuff a sock at Steamboat Rock
With Sarah Polley, Dr. Spock,
David Dinkins, Andie MacDowell,
Susan Nicely, and Colin Powell.
Our revelry in Beverly
Will take us all or severally
To Coos Bay or to Ketchikan
With Dr. Seuss and Gadge Kazan;
From there, with Anna Wintour, we
Could fly to Flint to light a tree,
And thence, with Richard Serra, tote
Some toys for tots in Terre Haute,
Where, jet-lagged to a fare-thee-well,
We'll have a nosh with Josh Mostel,
Or toast our toes at glowing brazier.
With Art Agnos and Cora Frazier.
We'll catch our breath in Hibbing, Minn.,
And ask some super neighbors in,
Like Paula Cooper, Mackey Sasser,
Naguib Mahfouz, Ira Glasser,
Bo Wulf, Los Lobos, Peter Coyote,
And folks from No. and So. Dakoty.
Next day, by Eggemoggin Reach,
We'll stay and hoist a noggin each
With Kenneth Branagh, Chris D'Amboise,
Anita Brookner, Amos Oz,
Daryl Hannah (sans duenna),
Harold Ramis, Neil MacKenna,
Baryshnikov, and Maxine Groffsky—
And good old Mieczyslaw Horszowski!

We end, old dears, in better cheer:
How sweetly Christmas comes this year!
Bright candles in the good king's square
Illuminate our midnight air.
Let peace descend, from alp to lowland—
Wesołych Świąt, chaps in Poland!
Fröhliche Weihnachten, West and East,
For all who flock to freedom's feast!
Happy *Nový Rok* (that's Czech), we say.
God bless us each this holiday!

AFTERWORD TO *Greetings, Friends!*:

This antique Christmas card, offered in two recent samples, is now in its fifty-fifth edition, which makes it the longest running verse-play on the boards. The opening staves appeared in The New Yorker *on December 24, 1932, and their author was the the amiable Frank Sullivan, who had no idea that he had just invented a form and an institution. Indeed, the verse had no successors until 1935, when Sullivan rolled up his sleeves and knocked off the second of what were to be forty more consecutive annual editions, greeting thousands of friends in tinkling, comical, sweetly scanning couplets that became a seasonal staple as pleasing and evocative as the candy cane. The current franchise-holder took over in 1976, after Sullivan's death, and immediately discovered that writing passable light verse is a snap, being no more difficult than dancing like Fred Astaire. After fourteen turns around the floor, he is still counting beats under his breath and trying not to look at his feet.*

Inquiries have been received (sometimes with the faint aroma of bribery wafting up from the envelope) about the criteria that determine one's chances of becoming a greetee on any given year. Qualifications, in ascending order of importance, are: friend of author; worthy person (Nobel Prize-winner, etc.); weird name (c.f., Lovely Billups, 1989); national or international celeb; rhyming name; metre-fitting name. Friends who have been ravished to find themselves paired with Dr. J or Pope John Paul on the right-hand side of a couplet may realize at this point that unrhymed *folks, over to the left, have attained the honor on pure merit. Deserving trochees (Tip O'Neill, Meryl Streep) and anapests (George F. Kennan) have been greeted again and again, while spondees (Bill Blass, Ed Koch, etc.) have lagged, since they require more thought. Some eminently deserving candidates (Judge Wapner heads this long list) have all stood, all uncalled, in the wings for many Christmases, because of a clunky handle. Making such choices, year after year, fills this rhymer with a sense of awe and absolute irresponsibility. A small private joke (not a rhyme) may now be revealed: In 1978, the author referred to the* Greetings, *within the verse, as a "dogged caterwaul," and two years later turned that into "catatonic doggerel." Both descriptions still apply.*

The NCMSB Report

PREFACE TO THE 1970 EDITION

This fifth edition is, to put it frankly, useless. Ever since this famous 1965 article first trumpeted clear warning of the findings of the National Cultural Manifestations Sampling Board, each annual reprinting has been snapped up in universities and bookstores across the land, yet that gratifying response has never been followed by the faintest evidence that anyone has changed his cultural patterns as a result. Today, we are not just slipping deeper into the cultural sink; we are down the drain. Every one of the dire predictions here has been precisely verified by events; the up-slashing curves made by extrapolations to 1970 in the original charts have proved in actuality to be even more sickeningly vertiginous. Even the mild hopes raised last year by the anti-cultural "good beginnings" of the Nixon Administration have been blasted. More recently, and only short weeks after President Nixon courageously invited Mr. Red Skelton to head the bill at a White House evening entertainment, the Chief Executive saw fit to journey to Philadelphia and there publicly and repeatedly clasp the hand of Leopold Stokowski! This example of unchecked cultural lasciviousness in the highest places suggests, to your editor at least, that there will not be a sixth edition of this document. Rome, it may be remembered, was also "cultured."—Ed.

"Wake up, America! The hour grows late, and it's time, high time, each one of us faced up to his responsibility to *do* something about the culture explosion. The facts are here. The only question that remains is whether we have the courage to face them!"

These bold, frightening words form the epilogue to the long-awaited 1200-page report of the National Cultural Manifestations Samplings Board: *The Crisis of Responsibility in an Age of Cultural Excess.* The volume, a sobering bedside-table "must" for every American who has recklessly plunged ahead with his old concert-, art-gallery-, and theatre-going habits, who has bought and read poetry and criticism in thoughtless profusion, who has even invited comparative abstainers to share his profligate evenings at art-film houses, now confirms in bullet-hard detail what far too many of us have only dared whisper: *The culture boom is out of control!* No longer can we ignore or fail to understand the fact that mankind, especially in such overleisured areas as the eastern United States, is approaching the point of *total* cultural saturation at a dizzying rate of mathematical progression. At this writing, the number of Americans undergoing some cultural experience is increasing at the rate of 97.2 per minute; to put it another way, 22,860,119 citizens never previously exposed to culture have experienced an initial cultural contact* since the closing moments of President Johnson's Inaugural Address! This makes all too clear the stubborn persistence of our old posture of laissez-faire frontier optimism toward cultural overgrazing (*"Have you practiced your scales today, Sam?"*—Booth Tarkington), and warns of the appalling task that now lies in the hands of our arts demographers.

The NCMSB Report, compiled over a fifteen-year period by two hundred and seven sociologists operating under a grant from the Saturday Review Foundation, places a powerful new weapon in the hands of a few profoundly discouraged cultural Cassandras. Only last year, the long-hoped-for Cultural Wilderness Bill, which would merely set aside a few million virgin acres in Kansas and Oklahoma from hi-fi and theatre-of-the-absurd depredation, was once again buried in congressional committee. Now, at least, solons will find it hard to dodge the sobering facts and statistics contained in the NCMSB Report's 426 tables and graphs. Consider, for instance, what lies immediately ahead for four of the East Coast's typical "culturally imploding" pockets.

*Not including *The Sound of Music.*—Ed.*

These sample areas—three square blocks in downtown New Hope, Pennsylvania; upper western Sullivan Street, in Manhattan; Madison Avenue from Sixty-eighth to Seventy-seventh Streets; and the South Shore of Long Island from East Hampton to Amagansett and inland to Springs—now contain an average of 522 culture-bound individuals per quarter acre, which is a gain of 297 per cent in four years. By 1970, their culture-practicers will have soared to a figure of 57 per square *foot*.* Culture "explosion"? Call it rather, a cataclysm.

Even when faced with these chilly figures, too many "free-culture" champions will probably fall back on their old shop-worn clichés: "We can always spread out," or "There's plenty of room out West." But *is* there? Let them read page 872 of the Report: "In December of 1964, no less than 31 families in Sioux Falls, South Dakota, gave or received Jackson Pollock jigsaw puzzles for Christmas. In the Greater Houston area, 712 families now have Aubrey Beardsley matchbooks or Ernest Trova kaleidoscopes on their coffee tables; 49 per cent of those same coffee tables are in the culturally tolerable free-form 'Art Shape.'" Clearly, the dangerous egalitarian cultural virus (*"I paint what I see."*—Eisenhower) is raging unchecked from coast to coast.

Let us proceed to a consideration, necessarily brief, of the NCMSB's samplings and tables, concentrating on those pertaining to the critical Eastern "culture megalopolis." The mere titles of these statistical cross-slicings reveal the profound cogitation and systemic rectitude that so distinguish the work of the Report's authors. Here are samplings in three areas of cultural hyperactivity:

1. *Vertical Culture:* "Weekend Hours Spent Waiting in Line Outside Guggenheim Museum; Outside Bergman/Chaplin/Bogart Film Festivals; in Ticket Line at Y.M.H.A. Poetry Center (cumulative)."

*A demographer recently attempting to check this figure in New Hope lost his ruler in the crush!—*Ed.*

2. *Visual Culture:* "Recognition of W. H. Auden/Susan Sontag/ Thomas Schippers Among Passing Street Pedestrians" (frequency per week).

3. *Active Culture:* "Summer Weekend Hours Devoted to Active Culture: (A) In Western History to 1900; (B) Since 1950, Among Sample Either Playing Softball with Larry Rivers in Amagansett or Tennis with Elia Kazan in Fairfield County."

Classicists will notice at once the absence of such tried-and-true tests of cultural activity as "Hours spent reading," "Hours spent in museums," "Hours spent practicing the recorder," etc. One of the NCMSB's most useful discoveries is the fact that these old standards are pathetically unreliable in statistical form, since they permit no evaluation of the depth of the culture subject's involvement in or understanding of his *Kulturwerk.* A man standing in front of Rembrandt's *The Anatomy Lesson* may be reminding himself to pick up some cold cuts at the delicatessen, and thus be at least momentarily culture-free; a man reading Burroughs' *Naked Lunch* may doze. By contrast, individuals in line outside a museum, or discussing or recognizing a cultural celebrity, are positively and inescapably *engagé,* in the Malrauxian sense. Consider, too, the startling unreliability of cultural *opinion* among samplees, as demonstrated in a puzzling and ultimately discarded NCMSB survey into audience understanding of Edward Albee's play *Tiny Alice.* Polled at regular intervals after the drama's initial appearance, playgoers at first divided almost equally, with 52.7% of those attending the previews claiming to understand the "meaning" of *Tiny Alice* and 47.3% admitting to confusion. By mid-December, 1964, the "Understand" group was strongly ascendant, claiming 80% of the total. A month later, however, there was a total rebalancing: 53.6% did *not* understand *Tiny Alice,* with the Understanders slipping down to 46.4%. By mid-February, 1965, only 11.1% still claimed to understand the play; nonunderstanding stood at a triumphant 88.9%. Extrapolating this curve, the experts predicted that total audience obscurity would be achieved a few minutes before noon on St.

Patrick's Day of the same year.* Clearly, "meaning" in culture has become déclassé and statistically anarchic, and must be discarded.

On, then, to the three initial tables—so similar, so implacable in their deadly upward arrow thrust toward impending total cultural chaos.

To break in for a moment: the inclusion of Mr. Schippers, the conductor, in Chart 2 is a remarkable tribute to the perceptiveness of the sample-takers and the over-all reliability of these statistics. Originally, the third cultural celebrity in this test was Mr. Leonard Bernstein. Certain inconsistencies in the figures puzzled the experts, however, and investigation disclosed the prevalence of a remarkable degree of Bernstein-hallucination among the culturally overexposed. Otherwise reliable interviewees swore to having seen the celebrated conductor on Fifty-seventh Street, at the Central Park Zoo, etc., at times when he was, in fact, in Hollywood or in the Berkshires. Mr. Schippers was then substituted. The scrupulous NCMSB pollsters also devised a number of "trick" questions that served to weed out culture-dazed subjects who were, for example, unable to tell the difference between Miss Susan Sontag and such other major culture figures as Susan Stein, Gloria Steinem, Stephen Sondheim, and Baby Jane Holzer. In the same fashion, they also eliminated celebrity-viewers who called the poet "Mr. Auden" or "W. H."—or, indeed, anything but "Wystan Auden."

Now, what do these three tables tell us? At first glance, statistically innocent readers or irresponsible cultural zealots may be tempted to state that we are on the threshold of three "impossible" eventualities—that the Eastern culture group will shortly be spending all 55 weekend hours (5 P.M. Friday to midnight Sunday) standing in line outside culture meccas; that Miss Sontag and Messrs. Auden and Schippers will be recognized by everyone

*In point of fact, it happened at 4:55 in the afternoon of March 16th, 1965. Mr. Albee, on hand at a matinee to make note of the occasion, presented a ceremonial bouquet of forget-me-nots to Mrs. Hallie Starbird, of Tonawanda, Md., who was the very last play-goer claiming to understand any part of *Tiny Alice*. Deeply touched, Mrs. Starbird thanked the playwright and then turned to a bystander and said, "Who was *that*?"—*Ed.*

CHART 1. WEEKEND HOURS SPENT WAITING IN LINE OUTSIDE
GUGGENHEIM MUSEUM; OUTSIDE BERGMAN/CHAPLIN/BOGART FILM
FESTIVALS; IN TICKET LINE AT Y.M.H.A. POETRY CENTER.

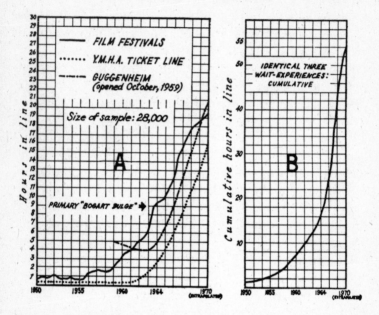

Note: In the appendix to the Report, the authors point out that the
foot of the weekend line outside the Guggenheim Museum has recently
come to within eighty-four feet of the foot of the line waiting for the
doors of the Metropolitan Museum to open, thus approaching the conditions of absolute culture-mix that now prevail in the infamous Third
Avenue cinema ghettos.*

*How charmingly innocent, how childlike in its minuscule anxieties, this
warning looks today, in the darker light of our 1970 knowledge! It was but two
or three months after the initial publication of the NCMSB report that the first
overt incidents along the Guggenheim-Metropolitan border were noted. Six
weeks later, despite herculean efforts by neutralist mediators, the matter had
exploded into the violent "Saturday War," which saw the exposure of the infamous Fifth Avenue pretzel-sellers' counterspy ring, the daring "Flying Nan-
nies'" raid on the Guggenheim spiral, and the reflexive ensuing capture and
cultural disarming of two hundred and sixty-three art lovers (including three
trustees) from the very top steps of the Met entranceway. The present state of
truce in the mid-Eighties blocks is, in the words of Hilton Kramer, "parlous,"
and the rival jostling hordes of cultural zealots that still throng the disputed
areas on weekends and holidays, flaunting their catalogues and whispering aesthetic excoriations, give scant promise of better times to come.—*Ed.*

CHART 2. RECOGNITION OF W. H. AUDEN/SUSAN SONTAG/THOMAS
SCHIPPERS AMONG PASSING STREET PEDESTRIANS.

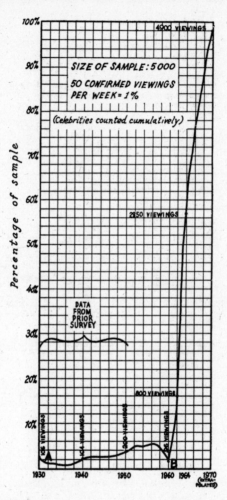

Note: (A) Miss Sontage as yet unborn; Mr. Schippers an infant. (B) Mr.
Auden in Vienna; Mr. Schippers in Spoleto.

CHART 3. SUMMER WEEKEND HOURS DEVOTED TO ACTIVE CULTURE.

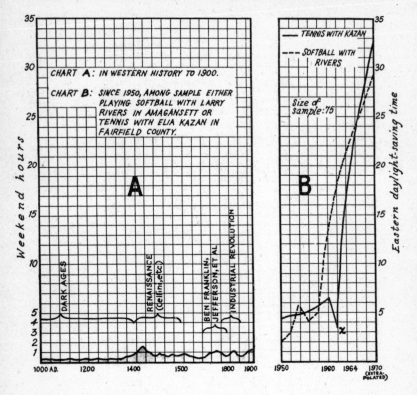

Note: (X) Mr. Kazan indisposed for four weeks with tennis elbow.

everywhere; and that Mr. Rivers and Mr. Kazan will have to spend *all* their summer daylight hours playing softball and tennis with culture companions. The answer: *exactly so!* To point out the obvious parallel, nuclear fission was also considered "impossible." We have arrived, in short, at our cultural Alamogordo.

Prolonged study of these tables allowed the Board scientists to theorize and then to confirm the existence among us of "cultural athletes"—individuals of almost unbelievable artistic stamina who were able, for example, to play tennis with Mr. Kazan on a Saturday morning, return to town and take their place in the queue outside a Chaplin Festival, and, while in line, recognize Miss Sontag, *en passant* across the street! From this was evolved the already famous Norman Cousins' Law: *"Culture is most practiced among the cultured."* This is possibly the most discouraging aspect of the entire crisis. It means that the very culture groups most in need of self-restraint and rigid culture-planning are most liable to cultural excess. These make up the shocking omnipresent hordes of the overcultured—the wan, hot-eyed families one sees alighting, with books, art catalogues, and guitars in hand, from their Volkswagens outside Lincoln Center and eagerly chattering as they hurry in to a fresh cultural experience that will "feed their habit."

The Board's ingenious development of the Mutchnick-Jamison Culture-Sensitivity Indicator permitted testing of some of this group against counter-samplings of a group on the cultural fringe and a group of cultural fellaheen (imported from Terre Haute, Indiana). The latter group had experienced no "Cult.-Stims." (reading the *Paris Review,* attending an Antonioni movie, buying a Bartók record, etc.) whatever; the middle group averaged less than one Cult.-Stim. weekly; the cultural élite (bitter misnomer!) was in need of at least five Cult.-Stims. weekly. The test measured physiological and emotional reactions to a typical Cult.-Stim.—the dropping of the name of Andy Warhol into conversation at 25-second intervals.

Chart 4 proves the *effects* of Cousins' Law. Note the total placidity and trustworthiness of Group A, the commoners. Note the beginnings, the faint warning twitches, of cultural excitement among Group B that accompany each Warhol-drop. And observe, at last, the *increasing* agitation, shortness of breath, and nail-biting among the culture addicts at each repeated "Warhol." Can there be any doubt remaining as to the horrid nature of the crisis that is upon us?

What is to be done to halt the culture explosion? The picture is ominously clouded. Preliminary glowing reports of the efficacy of the oral anti-culture pill developed in a crash program of research at the Orrick Laboratories seem to have been overop-

CHART 4. NAME-DROP SENSITIVITY AMONG THREE CULTURE GROUPS.

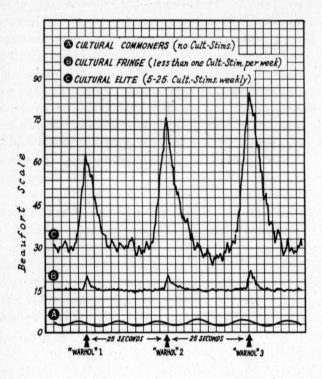

Ⓐ CULTURAL COMMONERS (no Cult.-Stims.)
Ⓑ CULTURAL FRINGE (less than one Cult.-Stim. per week)
Ⓒ CULTURAL ELITE (5-25. Cult.-Stims. weekly)

Beaufort Scale

"WARHOL" 1   ←—25 SECONDS—→   "WARHOL" 2   ←—25 SECONDS—→   "WARHOL" 3

timistic; test subjects now report that their initial sharp interest in the stock market, golf, etc., seems to flag after three to four months of daily pills. Fresh chemical experimentation has been undertaken. Plain old-fashioned cultural abstinence, by contrast, is now frowned upon by most social scientists, since it runs head-long into the widespread "culture is good for you" mystique, and occasionally leads to such aberrant practices as reading *Life* in darkened rooms, attending the Trans-Lux East alone, etc., and a resultant heavy load of guilt. Selective choice of healthful cultural substitutes, once urged by the New School for Social Research, has also proved ineffectual, simply because "Cultural substitutes tend to become cultural" (Susskind's Hypothesis). Each attempt by small, pioneer culture groups to switch to a culture substitute—i.e., cheering the New York Mets, watching

Busby Berkeley musicals on the "Late Show," playing whiffleball in Central Park—has led inexorably to a small cultural sub-explosion in that area, thus exacerbating the original problem.

At present, the only positive counter-measure appears to be disciplined adherence to the Cultural Rhythm System. Culture victims truly anxious to curb their old ways report considerable success as a result of daily temperature-taking and occasional weekend abstinence. They have learned to recognize the onset of the period of dangerous cultural hyperactivity, usually four to six days after the arrival of the *New York Review of Books* in one's mailbox. Temptation can often be avoided, especially on rainy weekends, by leaving town during this time, though trips to Westport, Tanglewood, etc., can lead to a "slip."

Realistically, however, it is asking too much of human nature to expect that such difficult voluntary sacrifices can bring the culture explosion to a halt. Next week, sixteen grim-faced top members of the NCMSB will pack bags, briefcases, and bulging cartons of blown-up data charts and take a train to Washington, where they have an appointment with congressional leaders.* Their message will be brief and fervent: The time has come for a federal program, backed up by the full power of the law, to put a stop to the culture explosion.

*Faugh!—*Ed.*

Fall Classic

(A Garland of Mixed Autumn Strophes Plucked after
an Evening of Aeschylus at the City Center, Followed
Too Quickly by an Afternoon of Mel Allen and the
World Series)

SCENE: *A mighty concrete* theatron, *triple-decked, brave with bunting
and bright with October sunshine. As the action commences, wealthy Athenians are still crowding the* diazoma *and the* klimakes *as they search
for their seats. In the center of the* orchestra *we see the altar, a mound
of earth topped with a rectangular slab of rubber. On either side of the
curving green* proskenion, *there is a* paraskenion, *in foul territory,
each containing a low shelter. From these shelters, from time to time,
appear heroes, arbiters, and godlings. Enter* MELALENDER, *a soothsayer.*

MELALENDER:

Hail, all hail, fandom, and thrice welcome be
To our vasty temple, House That Ruth Built,
Parnassian shrine and *skene* once more
To our unconstrain'd autumnal revels,
Where this day, not unwitnessed, shall unfold
A fresh renewal of full sacred rites,
Capstone, you might wanna say, of another
Great season of the great Attic pastime!

Soon, before thy to-be-affrighted eyes,
Will appear right fell fiends, Reds from the house

Of the Cincinnati, boldly to wrest,
If wrest they can, the cup of victory
From the hands of the bestrip'd-flannel-clad
Atticans, children of Hephaestus' seed,
And holders—yea, again!—of the precious,
Hotly fought junior-circuit gonfalon!

Fiends, I said, though sworn am I by my vows
To dread Pallas to strict neutrality,
And therefore I adduce, most hastily,
Refutal: that, for all I wot, these bold,
Hot-eyed hordes from Corn-belted Tartarus
May be good-conscienc'd, clean-limb'd fellows all,
Known for their reverence of hoary sires.
And now, pray, bend ears to this suasive plea.

CHORUS (*singing*):

How are ya fixed for blades,
  Striplings and elders?
How are ya fixed for blades,
  Ye chin-tress'd elders?
(Murmured counter-refrain):
Hear the hymn we spout
O'er the victim sounding:
Deft, soft agoran shout
Sense and will confounding!
Round the soul entwining
Without lute or lyre—
Souls in madness pining,
  Wasting as with fire . . .
(Full chorus, drowning out murmurs):
'Cause a worn-out blade makes shaving mighty tough!

MELALENDER
(speaking from a perch atop the paraskenion, *as, below him,* HEROES
disport themselves in various classic attitudes):

Behold, the White-Haired One doth retrieve
    The back-smit pitch, and, mounded high,
Wins again the multitude's fealty,
    So mighty is the grasp whereby,
Heaven-holpen, he doth whirl and throw,
    Secondward, southpawwise, the ball,
Seized there in midflight by the eagle
    Kubek, who now, with feather'd ease,
Wafts the sphere to the initial sack,
    The taloned Skowron's lair, who feasts
Thereupon, ending the uprising!
    Wrathy Pinson and guileful Post,
Their mouths befouled with dust, both lie dead!
    This twin killing—hear, O ye fans!—
Eraseth a hallowed mark, long 'graved
    'Pon the tablet-screeds of the sport,
For One-to-Six-to-Three double plays
    Executed by the home team
In the third inning of the first game,
    In the modern Periclean
Era, and how, Attic fans, about that!

(Scene shifts to an aperture in the paraskenion, *within which, in bored, easy postures, lounges an assemblage of* HEROES. *Enter a bow-legged, lantern-jawed, horny-handed* GHOST, *clad in faded flannels.)*

GHOST (*sepulchrally*):

Lo, what do I behold? My fellers all,
Mine erstwhile band of belaurelled heroes,
By o'erconfidence thus besapped again?
Do I roam scorned for naught? Awake and hear,
Ye fledglings of my brood! Look, look, alas,
Upon the shade of thy late Allfather,
So coldly bann'd by them that should have loved
The wise maunderings of his merry tongue.

Mark ye these wounds from which the heart's blood ran
When, not a year since, quite o'ercome we were
In the glutted haughtiness of our pride—
Felled by one mighty Mazeroskian
Four-ply swipe! Remember ye not that black day?
Awake, ye myrmidons! The footsore ghost
That once was Casey bids ye all arise!

HEROES (*severally*):

Cripes! . . .
           What do mine astonished orbs descry?
Is not . . .
          that ghastly spectre . . .
                    the Old Man?

GHOST:

Know ye me not, my babes, my famed platoons?
Are ye too drows'd in pride to heed my pain?
Ho, Duren! Ditmar! Come forth from hiding,
And right eftsoons shall I put all to rights!

(*Enter* FURIES, *symbols of Front Office Ingratitude*.)

GHOST (*seeing* FURIES):

Nay, 'tis not to be. That this skipper's helm
Is not now mine had quite beslipp'd my mind.
A troop of shadows, legions yet unborn,
Strangely hight The Mets, haply shall battle
For the Ol' Perfessor, cross yon reeky stream.
Revenge me! To the Polo Grounds, to Thrace,
To Lemnos, even to the Three-I League
Must I fly, these baying hounds at my heels.

FURIES:

Follow, seek him—round and round
Scent and snuff and scan the ground!

GHOST (*sinking*):

But who put my ketcher out in left field?

FURIES (*in a barbaric yawp*):

Houk! Houk! Houk!

CHORUS (*gladsomely*):

Grave priests of Acropolis,
   Youths in bosky glade,
Merchants in metropolis,
   Choose the Azure Blade!
       (*murmuring again*):
Round the soul entwining
   Runic words we wind,
Crumbling, cracking, mining
   The temple of the mind!
       (*shrilly*):
Oracles say, in their caves,
"Man, you never *had* such shaves!"

(*There is a sudden grumble of thunder, and the* CHORUS *exits hastily, casting nervous glances at the heavens. Enter* ORESTES *in the guise of a muscular blond right fielder. He falls to one knee and tensely executes some practice left-handed swings with a club.*)

ORESTES:

King Apollo, bright Hermes, Hercules,
And Hephaestian Foxx, look on me now!
A meagre boon humbly do I bespeak:
Send me this day but one fatted gopher
That I may thwack in Daedalian flight
Beyond the topmost rim of yon *skene*,

Heavenward ascending as sacrifice
To all thy ne'er-to-be-minished powers!

(Enter an eight-cylinder Chrysler Eccyclema, *a powder-blue job, with white-wall tires. It comes to a halt beside* ORESTES, *and from it steps the goddess* ATHENA, *who trips over her robe, then recovers herself.)*

ATHENA:

Far off I heard the clamor of thy cry,
Hummed on the wind instead of wings I came,
To charge thee, O not unseemly Earthling,
One full import-freighted question withal.

ORESTES *(grovelling)*:

Alack! I fear thy dreadful inquiry,
Great Queen. Methinks thou comest to punish me
For full many an impious blow struck
In o'ermuscled pride this half-twelvemonth past!
Dost thou come to thunder the heretofore
Murmured plaint of scribes—that in rank *hubris*
I have shaken the sixty-column'd shrine
Of the godling babe, the Sultan of Swat?

ATHENA:

Nay, arise, 'tis naught of that, sweet swinger,
Long since have you drear expiation done
In stare-ey'd nights unslept, in chances whiff'd,
In awesome pokes by stray zephyrs foul-blown.
'Tis but mine own small business brings me here,
One boon to beseech of *thee*. *(Simpering, she produces a tablet from her robes.)* Wouldst thou . . . uh . . .
Couldst thou, upon this tablet of purest
Wax, for Pallas, thy John Henry inscribe?

ORESTES (*obliging graciously*):

Sure thing, Queen—here. Now hie thee off this sward
Before yon dark-garbed minions, in dogged
Duty, to thee the old heave-ho impart.

(*He leads her away as she clutches the tablet happily to her breast.
Enter* CHORUS, *clearing its throat, but another growl of thunder causes
it to change its mind. It withdraws in confusion.*)

MELALENDER (*from his perch*):

Late it grows. Hespera's twin-hors'd chariot
   The Bronxian heavens hath quit.
Beclouded, shadow-smit, the blood-gouted tilt
   Unresolved before us sways!
Here, in ninth frame's nether half, the score, thick-tied,
   In Gordian gyves lies knotted.
Yet take heart, Atticans, for, lo, thy legions
   The enemy redoubts beclaw!
Whirlpits of despond whelm the Cincinnati!
   Loaded are the hassocks! One bingle
Shall waken shouts hereafter happy-thrilling,
   So don't go 'way, anybody!

SCENE: *A tense gathering of the Cincinnati at the central altar. Enter*
BROSNAEUS, *a bespectacled philosopher and fireman.*

BROSNAEUS:

Hither, and not unsummoned by thy call,
O Skipper, I come, heeding thy wigwag.
There, unfar from where stand we atremble,
My four eyes espy the deep-browed Yogi.
His awful mace, unbloodied yet, doth cleave
The void air—aswish doth he cleave it now,

His Ajax-like practice riffles withal!
But enough. Hand me the pill and withdraw
Thy melancholy visage dugoutward.

(The Cincinnati disperse, leaving BROSNAEUS *brooding alone. He soliloquizes.)*

They swarm, they swarm, these bestripèd tigers!
The loathly blood is dripping from their eyes.
Welladay! In my deep-furrowed mind's eye—
Unmyopic orb!—the foredoomed outcome
Full plainly I see: but brief minutes hence
Curv'd goat's horns my double dome shall adorn.
Aloed irony that I, a poet,
With an E.R.A. of three point oh four—
A true servant of Euterpe, Clio,
And their seven sisters of Helicon—
Should fall, dust-strewn, spittl'd, and dishonored,
To such an hairy band of thewy-skull'd
Picture-book perusers! Out upon it!
Now shall I cry for righting of this wrong.
Great Zeus, hear me! Thy thrall is in a jam.
Descend now, in omnipotence baring
Thine arm; perforate these anthropophages,
And succor this oppress'd twirler-Sophist!

(He pauses, looking upward, then shrugs.)

Nobody home. These dactyls have wearied
Even the Allhearer. Cooked now am I.

(He begins his warmup pitches. CHORUS, *seeing its chance, scrambles forward.)*

CHORUS *(chirpingly)*:

How are ya fixed for σπάθαι,
    Peloponnesians?

How are ya fixed for σπάθαι,
   Shave without lesions!
Please make sure you have ικανάι,
'Cause a worn-out σπάθη makes shavin' mighty χαλεπόν!

(A colossal lightning bolt descends from above the Grand Concourse, accompanied by an infuriated roar of thunder. CHORUS disappears in blue smoke. A cloudburst drops several billion gallons of wine-dark rain on the orchestra, scattering HEROES, arbiters, and Athenians, and quickly washing away the entire playing surface. Only BROSNAEUS and MELALENDER are left in view.)

MELALENDER:

Wow! There it *is*, fans—five-o'clock lightning!

BROSNAEUS (*his face turned up in wonder*):

This strain'd drama is now played out.
Somebody up there liketh me!

AFTERWORD TO *"Fall Classic"*

Time has so eroded this noble frieze that some archaeological footnotes must be appended. These warriors are engaged in the World Series of 1961, which was won by the Yankees over the Cincinnati Reds in five games. That was the season that Roger Maris hit sixty-one homers, breaking Babe Ruth's ancient record, and the year that Casey Stengel, after losing the previous World Series to Pittsburgh, was replaced by Ralph Houk as Yankee manager. Casey's Mets were as yet unborn, but the Furies did indeed follow him to the Polo Grounds—and beyond. In those tradition-ruled days, the Yankees were always in the World Series, and their broadcaster, Mel Allen, always handled the play-by-play, while Gillette paid for the singing commercials between innings—mellifluities that no longer echo in the porch of the national ear. Gone too are all these heroes.

The parody, inspired by a concurrent visit of the Greek Tragedy The-

atre repertory company to New York, was written just before the World Series began, and it contains an accurate sporting prediction—the "foredoomed outcome" envisaged by Brosnaeus. He, of course, is Jim Brosnan, the Cincinnati relief pitcher and author (his bullpen musings resulted in two good baseball books), who got a terrible going-over by the Yankee hitters; unsaved by the gods, he gave up nine hits, five runs, four walks, and two wild pitches in six innings of work. The writer's lot is not a happy one.

Adeste Brentano's!

(A Premonitory List of This Year's Yuletide Offerings
in Coffee-Table Literature)

On the Wing!

Eleven years ago, Holger T. Whitby, president of the Amalga-
mated Brass Company of America, quietly began photographing
houseflies with his family Brownie. Today, Mr. Whitby, no
longer a mere hobbyist, is recognized throughout the Nature
world as the photographic Audubon of insects in midair. Here
are over two hundred of his stunning full-page color portraits,
each in perfect focus, of midges, bluebottles, houseflies, ichneu-
mons, dung flies, mosquitoes, gnats, harlequin fruit flies, lady-
bugs, white-faced hornets, horseflies, seventeen-year locusts,
etc., all caught in full flight. Many exciting head-on views.
The text, which was written by Mrs. Whitby during her husband's convalescence from a recent bout of malaria, includes
many helpful hints about lens settings, camouflage, and antihis-
tamines that will permit you to take up this rewarding scientific
pursuit. $85.

The Tattoo Calendar

This handy, Phillips Brooks-style calendar is graced with 52
full-page photographs of masterpieces by the world's foremost
tattooists. Week by week, you will be charmed and fascinated
by a fresh, startling design etched in human skin, faithfully
reproduced here in full color. Included are Maori nose pat-

terns, a classic "Mother" heart of the Scollay Square Post-Impressionist school, Yokohama bicep flowers, and the Duke of Middlesex's celebrated ventral panorama of the Isle of Wight. The ideal gift for retired naval officers, dermatologists, etc. $12.50.

Christmas in the Senate

A joyous compendium of Yuletide sentiment from the hearts and tongues of America's most beloved senior solons. Includes eleven tributes to the Season of Good Will delivered in recent years on the floor of the Upper House just before Christmas adjournment, taken word for word from the pages of the *Congressional Record*. Some of the plums in this rich pudding are Senator Helms' memorable eulogium to the humble mistletoe, Senator Tower's inspired citation of Santa's reindeer during a debate on airline deregulation, and Senator Inouye's touching "A Boy's Christmas in Honolulu." The volume also contains an impeccable rerecording of Senator Borah's 1927 reading of "A Visit from St. Nicholas" to the Senate pageboys. $18.50.

Seven Roads to Springfield

It has fallen to the Cambridge historian P. L. J. W. Hogwought to remind Americans of the costly legacy we inherited from the bloody, unappreciated campaigns of Shays' Rebellion. Students of Armageddon will find harsh, meaningful parallels to subsequent and more publicized wars in this meticulous account of the tedious winter of 1786–87. You will not quickly forget the ironic significance of General Washington's famous murmured aside, the overturned chairs during the Parcheesi match at Worcester Court House, or the curious and nearly fatal oversight by General Benjamin Lincoln's hostler. Seventeen pull-out war maps, 827 pages, plus a foreword by the Military Affairs Editor of the *Wall Street Journal*. $30.

The Fireside Book of Bowling

For the first time, the complete lore, literature, reportage, great art, and humor of the world's most popular indoor sport! Vivid alleyside prose and poetry by Homer, Chaucer, Shakespeare, Pepys, Smollett, Jane Austen, Dickens, Dostoevski, Twain, Hemingway, Gide, Arthur Daley, et al., with kegling masterpieces of art by Veronese, Brueghel, Watteau, Renoir, Kandinsky, and others. It's all here, from that long-ago Golden Apple rolled by Eros, through Sir Francis Drake's nervy game of bowls at Plymouth Harbor, right down to the celebrated Jersey-side strike scored by Madeleine (Babe) LaFonza in the twelfth frame of the 1968 Middle States Women's Finals at the Bethlehem Bolo-Mat Lanes! A ten-strike of a book, exactly right for the sportsman or sportswoman in your family! $27.95.

My Friend Dusty

One cold November evening, lighthouse-keeper Eben Gorsuch went to his closet to take out his old herringbone tweed jacket, only to find that the entire left lapel had been eaten away during the summer. Such was Gorsuch's larval introduction to Dusty, the lovable and remarkably intelligent clothes moth (*Tinea pellionella*), who became his inseparable companion during the eleven months they shared on High Saliva, the desolate beacon that stands guard over the dreaded Mumbles. Cap'n. Gorsuch's personal diary, already a runaway best-seller, recounts the joys, the tears, and the constant surprises of a relationship rare in the annals of lepidoptera or the sea. Now readers may share in those morning "wakeup games," the search for Dusty's secret mitten, the housekeeper's departure, and the accidental but epochal discovery of moth-ratiocination during a midnight game of solitaire. Most affecting is Gorsuch's account of Dusty's last Michaelmas, a holiday that ended surprisingly when her master lit the candles for their festive *diner-à-deux*. In the words of Marlin Perkins, "This is an animal story not to be believed." Illustrated. $12.95.

Z-Along With Elvis

Now back in stock in the Americana Department is this eight-hour, eleven-tape (also available in quadruple-album LPs) intimate recording of Elvis Presley's "Book of Hours"—a private, perfect-fidelity taping of the King's breathings and stirrings as he slept through the night of March 6, 1971 in his own bed at Graceland. Rapt listeners can pick up unmistakable changes in respiration as Elvis shifts down to REM levels during the first and second hours, and the riveting moments when he clearly murmurs "dawg" (or possibly "augh!") in his sleep some fifty minutes before the first coughings and scratchings that accompany the return to morning consciousness. A collector's classic. $27.50 before December 1; then $45.

Pals from Out There

Does your dog ever stare fixedly at an invisible object just to one side of your head? Do your goldfish all change direction at the same instant, *for no reason?* Does your cat blink repeatedly when lying on an east-facing windowsill? Then they are pets from Outer Space—members of the millions of extra-terrestrials that now make up more than thirty-five percent of all domestic animals. Here, in one handy volume, are scientifically validated accounts of astounding extra-sensory behavior by dozens of dogs, cats, gerbils, parakeets, lizards, etc., on several continents. Read about "Mittens," the seven-year-old tortoiseshell from Highland Park, Ill., whose agitated yowlings and scratchings through September and early October of 1987 gave disregarded but uncannily accurate warnings of the coming stock market crash. Read about "Bugs Bunny," the three-pound Chinchilla rabbit who shares the cab with interstate trucker Marvin Hogarth on his long-distance runs, warning him miles in advance of radar speed traps by changes of eye color. Read in particular about "Mr. Ed," a six-year-old Samoyed, who disappeared from view on the day that his owners, Mr. and Mrs. E. L. Joyner, of Tallahassee, Fla., were changing residence. Five months and two days later, a footsore and weary Mr. Ed scratched at the door of the E. L. Joyners, of McCook, Nebraska—*absolutely no relation* to the Tallahassee Joyners, who had simply moved to a larger house (a modified Cape Cod, with patio) three blocks from their original home. These and other cases have been validated by John Francis Dowd, Professor of Mammalian Parapsychology at Oxford University. With photos. $18.75.

Ainmosni

Insomnia is my baby. We have been going steady for a good twenty years now, and there is no hint that the dull baggage is ready to break off the affair. Three or four times a week, somewhere between three and six in the morning, this faulty thermostat inside my head clicks to "On," raising my eyelids with an almost audible clang and releasing a fetid blast of night thoughts. Sighing, I resume my long study of the bedroom ceiling and the uninteresting shape (a penguin? an overshoe?) that the street light, slanting through the window, casts on the closet door, while I review various tedious stratagems for recapturing sleep. If I am resolute, I will arise and robe myself, stumble out of the bedroom (my wife sleeps like a Series E government bond), turn on the living-room lights, and take down a volume from my little shelf of classical pharmacopoeia. George Eliot, James, and Montaigne are Nembutals, slow-acting but surefire. Thoreau, a dangerous Seconal-Demerol bomb, is reserved for emergencies; thirty minutes in the Walden beanfield sends me back to bed at a half run, fighting unconsciousness all the way down the hall. Too often, however, I stay in bed, under the delusion that sleep is only a minute or two away. This used to be the time for Night Games, which once worked for me. I would invent a No-Star baseball game, painstakingly selecting two nines made up of the least exciting ballplayers I could remember (mostly benchwarmers with the old Phillies and Senators) and playing them against each other in the deserted stadium of my mind. Three or four innings of walks, popups, foul balls, and messed-up double plays, with long pauses for rhubarbs and the introduction of relief pitchers, would bring on catalepsy. Other nights, I would begin a solo round of golf (I am a terrible golfer) on some recalled course. After a couple of pars and a brilliantly holed birdie putt, honesty required me to begin playing my real game, and a long search for my last golf ball, horribly hooked into the cattails to the left of the sixth green, would uncover, instead, a lovely Spalding Drowz-Rite. In time, however, some perverse sporting instinct began to infect me, and my Night Games became hopelessly interesting. As dawn brightened the bedroom, a pinch-hitter would bash a line drive that hit the pitcher's rubber and rebounded crazily into a pail of water in the enemy dugout, scoring three runs and retying the game, 17–17, in the twenty-first inning; my drive off the fourteenth tee, slicing toward a patch of tamaracks, would be seized in midair by an osprey and miraculously dropped on the green, where I would begin lining up my putt just as the alarm went off. I had to close up the ballpark and throw away my clubs; I was bushed.

It was a Scottish friend of mine, a pink-cheeked poet clearly accustomed to knocking off ten hours' sleep every night, who got me into real small-hours trouble. He observed me yawning over a lunchtime Martini one day and drew forth an account of my ridiculous affliction. "I can help you, old boy," he announced. "Try palindromes."

"Palindromes?" I repeated.

"You know—backward-forward writing," he went on. "Reads the same both ways. You remember the famous ones: 'Madam, I'm Adam.' 'Able was I ere I saw Elba.' 'A man, a plan, a canal: Panama.' The Elba one is supposed to be about Napoleon. Here—I'll write it for you. You see, 'Able' backward is 'Elba,' and—"

"I know, I know," I snapped. "But what's that got to do with not sleeping? Am I supposed to repeat them over and over, or what?"

"No, that's no good. You must make up your own. Nothing to it. Begin with two-way words, and soon you'll be up to sentences. I do it whenever I can't sleep—'sleep' is 'peels,' of course—and in ten minutes I pop right off again. Never fails. Just now, I'm working on a lovely one about Eliot, the poet. 'T.

Eliot, top bard . . .' it begins, and it ends, 'drab pot toilet.' Needs a bit of work in the middle, but I'll get it one of these nights."

I was dubious, but that night, shortly after four, I began with the words. In a few minutes, I found "gulp plug" (something to do with bass fishing) and "live evil," and sailed off into the best sleep I had enjoyed in several weeks. The next night brought "straw warts" and "repaid diaper," and, in time, a long if faintly troubled snooze ("ezoons"). I was delighted. My palindromic skills improved rapidly, and soon I was no longer content with mere words. I failed to notice at first that, like all sedatives, this one had begun to weaken with protracted use; I was doubling and tripling the dose, and my intervals given over to two-way cogitation were stretching to an hour or more. One morning, after a mere twenty minutes of second shut-eye, I met my wife at the breakfast table and announced, "Editor rubs ward, draws burro tide."

"Terrific," she said unenthusiastically. "I don't get it. I mean, what does it *mean*?"

"Well, you see," I began, "there's this editor in Mexico who goes camping with his niece, and—"

"Listen," she said, "I think you should take a phenobarb to-night. You look terrible."

It was about six weeks later when, at five-fifteen one morning, I discovered the Japanese hiding in my pajamas. "Am a Jap," he said, bowing politely, and then added in a whisper, "Pajama." I slept no more. Two nights later, at precisely four-eleven, when "Repins pajama" suddenly yielded "Am a Jap sniper," I sprang out of bed, brewed myself a pot of strong coffee, and set to work with pencil and paper on what had begun to look like a war novel. A month later, trembling, hollow-eyed, and badly strung out on coffee and Dexamyl, I finished the epic. It turned out that the thing wasn't about a Japanese at all; it was a long tele-gram composed by a schizophrenic war veteran who had been wounded at Iwo Jima and was now incarcerated in some mental hospital. (This kind of surprise keeps happening when you are writing palindromes, a literary form in which the story line is controlled by the words rather than the author.) Experts have since told me that my barely intelligible pushmi-pullyu may be the longest palindrome in the English language:

> MARGE, LET DAM DOGS IN. AM ON SATIRE:
> VOW I AM CAIN. AM ON SPOT, AM A JAP SNIPER.
> RED, RAW MURDER ON G.I.! IGNORE DRUM.
> (WARDER REPINS PAJAMA TOPS.) NO MANIAC,
> MA! IWO VERITAS: NO MAN IS GOD.
> —MAD TELEGRAM

My recovery was a protracted one, requiring a lengthy vacation at the seashore, daily exercise, warm milk on retiring, and eventually a visit to the family psychiatrist. The head-candler listened to my story ("Rot-cod . . ." I began), then wrote out a prescription for a mild sedative (I murmured, "slip pils") and swore me to total palindromic abstinence. He told me to avoid Tums, Serutan, and men named Otto. "Only right thinking can save you," he said severely. "Or rather, *left-to-right* thinking."

I tried, I really tried. For more than a year, I followed the doctor's plan faithfully, instantly dropping my gaze whenever I began to see "POTS" and "KLAW" on traffic signs facing me across the street, and plugging away at my sleepy-time books when I was reafflicted with the Big Eye. I had begun to think that mine might be a total cure when, just two weeks ago, nodding over *Walden* again, I came upon this sentence: "We are conscious of an animal in us, which awakens in proportion as our higher nature slumbers. It is reptile and sensual, and perhaps cannot be wholly expelled. . . ."

"Ah-ha!" I muttered, struck by the remarkable pertinence of this thought to my own nocturnal condition. Thoreau himself had said it; I could never quite escape. To prove the point, I repeated my exclamation, saying it backward this time.

I did not entirely give way to my reptile. Remembering my near-fatal bout with the telegram, I vowed to limit myself entirely to revising and amplifying existing palindromes—those famous chestnuts recited to me by my Scottish friend. The very next night, during a 4 A.M. rainstorm, I put my mind to "A man, a plan, a canal: Panama." Replacing de Lesseps with a female M.I.T. graduate, I achieved "A *woman,* a plan, a canal: Pana-mowa," which was clearly inadequate; she sounded more like a ballerina. Within a few minutes, however, a dog trotted out of the underbrush of my mind—it was a Pekinese—and suddenly redesigned the entire isthmus project: "A dog, a plan, a canal: pagoda." I went to sleep.

Napoleon led me into deeper waters. Bedwise by night light, I envisioned him as a fellow-sufferer, a veteran palindromist who must have been transfixed with joy to find the island of his first exile so brilliantly responsive to his little perversion. But what if the allies had marooned him on a *different* island in 1814? Various possibilities suggested themselves: "A dum reb was I ere I saw Bermuda," "No lava was I ere I saw Avalon," "Lana C. LaDaug was I ere I saw Guadalcanal." None would do; the Em-peror's aides, overhearing him, would conclude that the old boy had fallen victim to aphasia. A night or two later, I replaced Boney on Elba and retinued him with a useful and highly di-versified staff of officers and loyal friends—a Rumanian, a fe-male camp follower, a Levantine, and a German. These accompanied the Emperor by turns during his habitual evening walks along the cliffs, each feigning awe and delight as the im-promptu musing of the day fell from his lips. "Uncomfortable was I ere I saw Elba, Trofmocnu," he confessed to the first. To the female, smiling roguishly and chucking her under the chin, he murmured, "Amiable was I ere I saw Elba, Ima." The next evening, made gloomy by the rabbinical sidekick, he changed to "Vegetable was I ere I saw Elba, Tegev." He cheered up with the burly Prussian, declaiming, "Remarkable was I ere I saw Elba, Kramer!" but, finding the same man on duty the following night (the list had run out, and new duty rosters were up), he reversed himself, whining, "*Un*remarkable was I ere I saw Elba, Kramer, *nu?*"

That seemed to exhaust Elba (and me), and during the wee hours of last week I moved along inevitably to "Madam, I'm Adam." For some reason, this jingle began to infuriate me. (My new night journeys had made me irritable and suspicious; my wife seemed to be looking at me with the same anxious expression she had worn when I was fighting the Jap sniper, and one day I caught her trying to sneak a telephone call to the psychiatrist.) Adam's salutation struck me as being both rude and uninformative. At first, I attempted to make the speaker more civilized, but he resisted me: "Good day, Madam, I'm Adam Yaddoog," "Howdy, Madam, I'm Adam Y. Dwoh," "*Bonjour,* Madam, I'm Adam Roujnob." No dice. Who *was* this surly fellow? I determined to ferret out his last name, but the first famous Adam I thought of could only speak after clearing his throat ("*Htims,* Madam, I'm Adam Smith"), and the second after falling down a flight of stairs ("*Yksnilomray!* . . . Madam, I'm Adam Yarmolinsky"). Then, at exactly six-seventeen yesterday morning, I cracked the case. I was so excited that I woke up my wife. She stared at me, blurry and incredulous, as I stalked about the bedroom describing the recent visit of a well-known congressman to Wales. He had gone there, I explained, on a fact-finding trip to study mining conditions in the ancient Welsh collieries, perhaps as necessary background to the mine-safety bills now pending in Washington. Being a highly professional politician, he boned up on the local language during the transatlantic plane trip. The next morning, briefcase and homburg in hand, he tapped on the door of a miner's cottage in Ebbw Vale, and when it was opened by a lady looking very much like Sara Allgood in "How Green Was My Valley," he smiled charmingly, bowed, and said, "*Llewopnotyalc,* Madam, I'm Adam Clayton Powell."

When I got home last night, I found a note from my wife saying that she had gone to stay with her mother for a while. Aware at last of my nearness to the brink, I called the psychiatrist, but his answering service told me that he was away on a month's vacation. I dined forlornly on hot milk and Librium and was asleep before ten . . . and awake before three. Alone in bed, trembling lightly, I restudied the penguin (or overshoe) on the wall, while my mind, still unleashed, sniffed over the old ashpiles of canals, islands, and Adams. Nothing there. Nothing, that is, until seven-twelve this morning, when the beast unearthed, just under the Panama Canal, the small but glittering prize, "Suez . . . Zeus!" I sat bolt upright, clapping my brow, and uttered a great roar of delight and despair. Here, I could see, was a beginning even more promising than the Jap sniper. Released simultaneously into the boiling politics of the Middle East and the endless affairs of Olympus, I stood, perhaps, at the doorway of the greatest palindromic adventure of all time—one that I almost surely would not survive. "No!" I whimpered, burying my throbbing head beneath the pillows. "No, no!" Half smothered in linen and sleeplessness, I heard my sirens reply. "On!" they called. "On, on!"

FOR THE BEST IN PAPERBACKS, LOOK FOR THE 🐧

In every corner of the world, on every subject under the sun, Penguin represents quality and variety—the very best in publishing today.

For complete information about books available from Penguin—including Pelicans, Puffins, Peregrines, and Penguin Classics—and how to order them, write to us at the appropriate address below. Please note that for copyright reasons the selection of books varies from country to country.

In the United Kingdom: For a complete list of books available from Penguin in the U.K., please write to *Dept E.P., Penguin Books Ltd, Harmondsworth, Middlesex, UB7 0DA.*

In the United States: For a complete list of books available from Penguin in the U.S., please write to *Dept BA, Penguin,* Box 120, Bergenfield, New Jersey 07621-0120.

In Canada: For a complete list of books available from Penguin in Canada, please write to *Penguin Books Ltd, 2801 John Street, Markham, Ontario L3R 1B4.*

In Australia: For a complete list of books available from Penguin in Australia, please write to the *Marketing Department, Penguin Books Ltd, P.O. Box 257, Ringwood, Victoria 3134.*

In New Zealand: For a complete list of books available from Penguin in New Zealand, please write to the *Marketing Department, Penguin Books (NZ) Ltd, Private Bag, Takapuna, Auckland 9.*

In India: For a complete list of books available from Penguin, please write to *Penguin Overseas Ltd, 706 Eros Apartments, 56 Nehru Place, New Delhi, 110019.*

In Holland: For a complete list of books available from Penguin in Holland, please write to *Penguin Books Nederland B.V., Postbus 195, NL-1380AD Weesp, Netherlands.*

In Germany: For a complete list of books available from Penguin, please write to *Penguin Books Ltd, Friedrichstrasse 10-12, D-6000 Frankfurt Main I, Federal Republic of Germany.*

In Spain: For a complete list of books available from Penguin in Spain, please write to *Longman, Penguin España, Calle San Nicolas 15, E-28013 Madrid, Spain.*

In Japan: For a complete list of books available from Penguin in Japan, please write to *Longman Penguin Japan Co Ltd, Yamaguchi Building, 2-12-9 Kanda Jimbocho, Chiyoda-Ku, Tokyo 101, Japan.*

FOR THE BEST IN PAPERBACKS, LOOK FOR THE ⓟ

☐ **THE GAME**
Ken Dryden

The veteran of eight years as goalie for the Montreal Canadiens, Ken Dryden reveals the texture of hockey—from the fundamentals to the rivalries and camaraderie—as only an athlete can.

"Extraordinarily insightful"—*Philadelphia Inquirer*
248 pages   ISBN: 0-14-007412-0   **$6.95**

☐ **THE LONG SEASON**
Jim Brosnan

An inside account of the 1959 baseball season by a veteran National League pitcher, *The Long Season* presents an honest look at the game and many of its greatest stars, including Stan Musial, Hank Aaron, and Willie Mays.

"Probably the best factual book in the literature of baseball"—*The New Yorker*
278 pages   ISBN: 0-14-006754-X   **$6.95**

☐ **THE SHORT SEASON**
The Hard Work and High Times of Baseball in the Spring
David Faulkner

In a collection of anecdotes, stories, and interviews, David Faulkner captures the sunny, all-things-are-possible atmosphere, the conditioning and carousing, of the "Grapefruit League."

"A vivid, exciting account . . . David Faulkner is the most engaging baseball writer since Roger Angell."—*Philadelphia Inquirer*
276 pages   ISBN: 0-14-009850-X   **$6.95**

☐ **CHAMPION**
Joe Louis: Black Hero in White America
Chris Mead

This is a masterful biography of Joe Louis the man—more than the Heavyweight Champion of the World, Louis was the most recognized black American of his time and a dignified symbol of hope and achievement.

"A valuable addition to American social history"—Robert Creamer, *Washington Post Book World*   330 pages   ISBN: 0-14-009285-4   **$6.95**

☐ **WHY TIME BEGINS ON OPENING DAY**
Thomas Boswell

From an affectionate and analytical perspective, veteran sports writer Thomas Boswell offers a penetrating look at the traditions, teams, ballparks, and games that make up the national pastime and inevitably the American grain as well.

"The writing is fresh, enthusiastic, and joyous."—*New York Times Book Review*   298 pages   ISBN: 0-14-007661-1   **$6.95**

FOR THE BEST IN PAPERBACKS, LOOK FOR THE 🐧

☐ **CAN'T ANYBODY HERE PLAY THIS GAME?**
Jimmy Breslin

Breslin's celebrated account of the New York Mets' first year of life—a year that produced a record number of losses and an unforgettable collection of oddballs— is a jubilant toast to the tenacity of the human spirit.

"Jimmy Breslin has written a history of the Mets, preserving for all time a remarkable tale of ineptitude, mediocrity, and abject failure."—Bill Veeck
124 pages   ISBN: 0-14-006217-3   **$5.95**